Praise for *Martin Luther: Preacher of the Cross*

Here is insight to do a daily ministry of teaching, challenging, and comforting that truly cares for souls. Pastors facing requests to be all things to all people will find in this guide a basis for discerning what is important from what is not. They will find focus and energy to fulfill their God-appointed calling.

—Dr. Mark C. Mattes
Professor of Philosophy and Theology
Grand View University, Des Moines, Iowa

John Pless has distilled twelve years of teaching experience into a valuable and insightful book. Theology is a practical aptitude (*Theologia est habitus practicus*), especially for Lutheran pastors. Pless demonstrates the integration of heart and mind, faith and knowledge, experience and pastoral care by examining "how Luther put his evangelical theology to work in actual cases of pastoral care" (14). Pastoral care is spiritual warfare against the evil one. It is time we reclaimed that focus and seriousness in soul care. We can learn much from the "how" and "what" of Luther's Christ-centered preaching.

—Rev. Paul J Cain
Pastor of Immanuel Lutheran Church, Sheridan, Wyoming
Editor of *Liturgy, Hymnody, and Pulpit Quarterly Book Review*

Reliable markers are life saving to navigate any jungle. As Lutherans in Africa, we are grateful for the clear and joyful song from that Wittenberg nightingale, dispelling fear of eternal damnation by vocalizing the accomplishments of the One who overcame sin, death, and devil for the entire world. In this practical study, crucial highlights from Luther's pastoral treasury masterfully guide readers, whetting the appetite for more. This is a most suitable handbook for all who study and teach theology.

—Dr. Wilhelm Weber
Rector of Lutheran Theological Seminary in Tshwane
Bishop of the Lutheran Church in Southern Africa

John Pless shows with many examples and rich quotations from Luther how the reformer brought consolation to troubled consciences and set them right with God through the encounter with both Law and Gospel. This is an important book for those who care to mine Luther's insights in assisting them in pastoral care for their own lives and the lives of those entrusted to them.

—Prof. Dr. Hans Schwarz
Full Professor of Systematic Theology and Contemporary Theological Questions
Institute for Evangelical Theology, University of Regensburg, Germany

The craft of responsible soul care in our confusing times is greatly enriched by *Martin Luther: Preacher of the Cross*—a master class in the care of souls. John Pless's long pastoral experience and years of Luther studies provide a rich storehouse of Christocentric treasures from which contemporary pastors may draw both inspiration and insight for faithful and sensitive care of the sheep and lambs of Christ.

—Rev. Harold L. Senkbeil, STM, DD
Executive Director for Spiritual Care
DOXOLOGY: The Lutheran Center for Spiritual Care and Counsel

The precious art of communicating Law and Gospel in pastoral situations, such as distress, despair, illness, and death, is here compactly presented with the wisdom of experience, not only John Pless's years as pastor and professor, but also and especially Martin Luther's experience of prayer and trial as seen in his catechisms and "Letters of Spiritual Counsel." The Luther quotations are ample and apt, the secondary bibliography judicious and current.

—Dr. Paul Rorem
Benjamin B. Warfield Professor of Ecclesiastical History
Princeton Theological Seminary, Princeton, New Jersey

Doctrine and life, for Luther, belong inseparably together. Therefore, the care of souls is not a distinct discipline or technique for Luther; it is not a theory but an activity. This book by John Pless is an introduction to this activity by leading the reader through the various areas of the care of souls as it is given and received. Due to the many citations, Luther himself speaks, and in this way the reader discovers what we as Christians through Christ are and what Christ has done for us and presently through Word and Sacrament does to us. This is a book that, in its clarity, serves not only to educate pastors but also to edify the congregation.

—Prof. Dr. Reinhard Slenczka, DD
Professor Emeritus
Erlangen Faculty of Theology, Erlangen, Germany

This book offers a sensitive, insightful assessment of how Luther opened Scripture to the daily life experiences of individual acquaintances and his Wittenberg congregation. Pless's judicious selection of texts from concrete contexts provides a bridge over the centuries that models application of God's Word today.

—Dr. Robert A. Kolb
Professor of Systematic Theology Emeritus
Concordia Seminary, St. Louis, Missouri

Martin Luther: Preacher of the Cross opens to us the heart of the Reformation, including the use of sacraments and vocation, and succeeds in revealing the rich practical and theological resources at our church's disposal for comforting troubled souls from cradle to grave. The insights Professor Pless offers on marriage and care of the poor alone are worth the price, to say nothing of how Luther teaches our faith properly to fight against the attacks of sin, death, and devil. This is a great, useful, and inspirational book that sets a new standard for the pastoral care of the future. It is not to be missed!

—Dr. Steven D. Paulson
Professor of Systematic Theology
Luther Seminary, St. Paul, Minnesota

This book is a significant contribution to pastoral theology. Not only do we read much about Luther, but this book also beckons pastors to follow suit. Pastors are entrusted with the task of being caretakers of people's troubled consciences and struggles in life; this book will again bring to the attention the truth and seriousness of pastoral care and ministry.

—Dr. Klaus Detlev Schulz
Chairman, Pastoral Ministry and Missions
Supervisor of PhD Missiology Program, Dean of Graduate Studies
Concordia Theological Seminary, Fort Wayne, Indiana

Martin Luther

Preacher of the Cross

MARTIN LUTHER

Preacher of the Cross

A Study of Luther's Pastoral Theology

John T. Pless

CONCORDIA PUBLISHING HOUSE · SAINT LOUIS

Published by Concordia Publishing House
3558 S. Jefferson Avenue, St. Louis, MO 63118-3968
1-800-325-3040 • www.cph.org

Scripture quotations are the author's translation.

Quotations from the Book of Concord with the abbreviation K-W are from Robert Kolb and Timothy J. Wengert, eds. *The Book of Concord: The Confessions of the Evangelical Lutheran Church* (Minneapolis: Fortress Press, 2000). Reproduced by permission of Augsburg Fortress.

The quotations marked AE are from Luther's Works, American Edition (56 vols.; St. Louis: Concordia Publishing House and Philadelphia: Fortress Press, 1955–86).

Manufactured in the United States of America
Library of Congress Cataloging-in-Publication Data

Pless, John T., 1953-
Martin Luther : preacher of the cross : a study of Luther's pastoral theology / John T. Pless.
pages cm
Includes bibliographical references and index.
ISBN 978-0-7586-1113-0 (alk. paper)
1. Luther, Martin, 1483-1546. 2. Pastoral theology--Lutheran Church--History--16th century. 3. Luther, Martin, 1483-1546--Correspondence. I. Title.

BR333.5.P32P54 2013
253--dc23

2013024121

---

6 7 8 9 10 11 12 32 31 30 29 28 27 26

Table of Contents

Abbreviations

AE	Luther, Martin. *Luther's Works*. American Edition. Volumes 1–30: Edited by Jaroslav Pelikan. St. Louis: Concordia, 1966–76. Volumes 31–55: Edited by Helmut Lehmann. Philadelphia/Minneapolis: Muhlenberg/Fortress, 1957–86. Volumes 56–75: Edited by Christopher Boyd Brown. St. Louis: Concordia, 2009–.
K-W	Kolb, Robert, and Timothy J. Wengert, eds. *The Book of Concord: The Confessions of the Evangelical Lutheran Church*. Minneapolis: Fortress Press, 2000.
LC	Large Catechism
SC	Small Catechism
Tappert	Tappert, Theodore. *Luther: Letters of Spiritual Counsel*. Philadelphia: The Westminster Press, 1960.
WA	*D. Martin Luthers Werke: Kritische Gesamtausgabe*. 73 vols. in 85. Weimar: H. Böhlau, 1883–.
WA Br	*D. Martin Luthers Werke: Briefwechsel*. 18 vols. Weimar: H. Böhlau, 1930–.
WA TR	*D. Martin Luthers Werke: Tischreden*. 6 vols. Weimar: H. Böhlau, 1912–21.

Foreword

I shall never forget a graduate seminar I attended on Luther's commentary on 1 Corinthians 15. The sainted Luther scholar Dr. Ulrich Asendorf would enter the classroom daily. We'd come to order quietly in the face of his genteel but Teutonic authority. He'd lecture on the text before us for about twenty minutes, and then, with classic Socratic skill, he would pull us into Luther's text and argument with such thoroughness, such erudition and clarity, that his burning passion for Martin Luther and the great reformer's incomparable insight into the Gospel of the resurrected Christ burned deeply into my heart. Luther's *extra nos* theology of the cross, insight into the blindness of human reason and the depth of the meaning of the resurrection, and his penetrating understanding of St. Paul all struck me profoundly. I wanted more, much more.

Luther's understanding of the implications of the resurrection of Christ became the mainstay of my pastoral care in the midst of death and dying henceforth. Paul calls Christ the "firstfruits" of those who sleep (1 Corinthians 15:20). He's risen, and there is more coming after Him! Christ as the "Head" of the Body is born unto eternal life; and just as in natural childbirth, the head comes only with difficulty, but then the body follows easily. So shall it be with our own resurrection! In fact, says Luther, death shall seem but a brief, refreshing nap. And because the hard part is done with Christ's own resurrection, it is as though we are all but raised ourselves—yes, with only but a toe yet dangling in the grave! Said Asendorf to us, "We do not say 'Back to Luther.' We say 'Forward to Luther!' Luther is so far ahead of us in understanding Christ and the Gospel that we have not caught up to him yet!"

While I read John Pless's *Martin Luther: Preacher of the Cross*, my heart leaped with the same kind of joy once stirred by Asendorf—joy in the clarity, the penetrating profundity, and the fundamental, simple, practical utility of Luther's pastoral writings.

Luther once wrote: "A drunkard leads the thirsty, and both are lost" (AE 28:66). Years ago, a retiring ELCA clergyman, a gem of a human being, gave me the pick of his library. It was packed with psychological volume after volume. The dominant theme: pastor as therapist, counselor, and psychological healer. Don't get me wrong—I rejoice in First Article gifts and have very high regard for the discipline of psychology and professional pastoral counseling. The library of that retiring pastor represented the dominant approach to practical theology of the 1950s and well into the late 1980s. But *Seelsorge* is not junior psychology. Care of souls is a profound theological discipline that requires deep and acquired insight into the human condition, especially regarding what the Bible has to say about God's dealing with humankind through the cross of Jesus. Gaining this competence to care for souls comes only with deep trials, which force us to prayer, meditation, and the Gospel itself. In the midst of such *tentatio*, there is no better guide than Luther. Without him, Lutheran care for souls is impoverished, even lost. Drunk with therapeutic methodology, we thirsted (often without realizing it) for what was missing—a thoroughgoing Lutheran care for souls as a theological craft.

This book is a profound indication that the craft is experiencing a renaissance among us, even in our own time. "Forward to Luther!"

Pastor Matthew C. Harrison
Assistant Pastor, Village Lutheran Church—Ladue, Missouri
President, The Lutheran Church—Missouri Synod
Commemoration of the Death of Luther, February 18, 2013

Preface

In less than four years, Lutherans around the world will celebrate the five hundredth anniversary of the posting of the Ninety-Five Theses, marking the beginning of the Reformation. Often significant Reformation anniversaries have yielded diverse pictures of Luther reflecting cultural and theological trends of the day. I doubt that 2017 will be little different. Some in our pluralist context are even suggesting that the five hundredth anniversary of the Reformation ought to give the world a "non-confessional Luther." Whatever images of Luther emerge in the next few years, we should not forget that Luther was a pastor who aimed to give sinners knowledge in the certainty of God's grace and mercy through faith in Christ Jesus. Luther went about that task with vigor and clarity, determined to know nothing but Christ crucified, to use the words of the apostle Paul (2 Corinthians 2:2).

This book, *Martin Luther: Preacher of the Cross*, was conceived in the course of serving as a pastor and as a teacher of future pastors. In my years of service as a pastor, Luther was a constant source of inspiration, curiosity, and challenge. His witness found its way into the sermons I preached, the Bible classes I taught, and the pastoral conversations I had. My interest in Luther was certainly academic as I read and studied his writings, took classes, wrote articles, and led seminars. But the fascination with Luther was more than intellectual; it was fueled by the necessity to preach Christ, articulating the truth that it is only through faith in Him that human beings have life with God in the forgiveness of sins. When I accepted the call to teach practical theology at Concordia Theological Seminary in Fort Wayne, Indiana, in 2000, I was determined to use Luther's writings to teach the care of souls. In large part, this book represents a dozen years of attempting to do just that in classes taught on campus, in extension courses for pastors throughout the United States, and, in the last three years, in intensive term courses taught at the Lutheran Theological Seminary in Tshwane (Pretoria), South Africa. It was and is my conviction that the more pastors are grasped by Luther's theology, the stronger their preaching of repentance and faith will be. Luther's theology is nothing if it is not realistic—both about human sin and unmerited divine mercy in Christ. This realism will serve pastors seeking to minister faithfully to Christ's sinful, yet holy flock.

Books such as this one are never merely the product of their author. Authors pour into their writings much of what they have received from those who have gone before them and those who are companions along the way. Wrapping up this project brings to mind several teachers and mentors, including Dr. James Schaaf, with whom I studied Luther's writings at Trinity Lutheran Seminary in Columbus, Ohio; Dr. Norman E. Nagel, who led me ever deeper into Luther's confession of Christ while I served with him at the Chapel of the Resurrection at Valparaiso University; Dr. Robert Preus, who helped me understand the connection between Luther and the Lutheran Confessions; and Dr. Kenneth F. Korby, who embodied Luther's theology in his own work of pastoral care. Others whose lives and work have intersected with mine and each in his own way has helped me think more clearly about Luther and what he has to say to pastors today include Michael Albrecht, Oswald Bayer, Jacob Corzine, Lowell Green, Matthew C. Harrison, Robert Kolb, Jason Lane, Mark C. Mattes, James Nestingen, Oliver Olson, Steven Paulson, and Bryan Wolfmueller. I am especially grateful to faculty colleagues Dr. Naomichi Masaki and Dr. Roland Ziegler for their collaboration and friendship in the day-to-day life of teaching. It has been a delight to join them in leading our "extra-curricular" Luther Seminar for outstanding students who have demonstrated a competency in Luther studies. It is a deep joy to know that many of these students are making their own contributions as pastors and scholars in the Church. I am also appreciative for my fellow seminar members at the 12th International Congress for Luther Research meeting in Helsinki, Finland, in August 2012 for the constructive suggestions given when I presented an overview of this book. Their insights and encouragement assisted me in bringing this project to completion.

I would also like to record my appreciation for the Rev. Scot Kinnaman and his staff at Concordia Publishing House for their helpfulness throughout the process of bringing this book to publication. Their kindness and patience along with their technical skills have enabled me to see this work to its conclusion. I am deeply grateful to President Matthew C. Harrison for this thoughtful Foreword, which reflects his commitment to ensure that the voice of Martin Luther remains heard in our Church and beyond.

I doubt that I would have written this book were it not for my experiences as a pastor at University Lutheran Chapel in Minneapolis from 1983–2000. This vibrant congregation experienced much turmoil and pain in 2012 when they were forced out of the chapel that was their home. They have demonstrated faithfulness and patience under the cross. I dedicate *Martin Luther: Preacher of the Cross* to them as even now they give evidence of resilience that is only possible because of the Gospel.

John T. Pless
Day of J. K. Wilhelm Löhe, Pastor
January 2, 2013
Concordia Theological Seminary
Fort Wayne, Indiana

INTRODUCTION

Learning the Art of Pastoral Care from Luther

Luther: The Pastoral Reformer

Martin Luther was not a parish pastor in the conventional sense of the term. His calling was that of a university professor. Yet he was intimately engaged in the care of souls. The history of the Reformation reveals how this world-changing movement erupted out of Luther's engagement with penitents whose minds were ensnared with misshaped notions of repentance and whose hearts were uncertain whether or not God's merciful favor would avail for their souls in the hour of death. Luther did not set out to reform the Church as he did to reform preaching. Preaching in this broad sense includes not only the sermon preached in the context of the liturgy but the whole spectrum of pastoral acts by which the word of divine promise is handed over to sinners—the speaking of the Gospel, Baptism, Absolution, the Lord's Supper, and Christian counsel and consolation, to name the most obvious. The Reformation was indeed radical in that it trickled down into every aspect of churchly life and piety. Nothing would be left untouched. This was especially true of pastoral care.

This book looks into Luther's practice of pastoral care. His insights, gleaned from his lifelong endeavor to bring consolation to troubled consciences by setting them right with God through the justifying Word that they might live in the freedom of faith toward their Creator and in the generosity of love toward the neighbor, provide lessons that might assist contemporary pastors. The twentieth century witnessed significant shifts in pastoral care away from a theological discipline to a psychological orientation. This shift is aptly summarized in the subtitle of E. Brooks Holifield's magisterial study, *A History of Pastoral Care in America: From Salvation to Self-Realization*. In our most recent past, theology was made subservient to the social sciences. Therapeutic concerns dominated theological realities. Pastors were shaped according to a clinical model, and more often than not, the rich pastoral wisdom of the past was viewed as suspiciously premodern. Works by scholars such as Thomas Oden and Andrew Purves[1] have called for a retrieval of classical models of pastoral care. Following their lead, this volume examines representative aspects of Luther's pastoral care manifested in his dealings with specific situations and people. *Martin Luther: Preacher of the Cross* is not a book about Luther's doctrine of the ministry. There are plenty of scholarly books and articles that have investigated that topic.[2] Rather, this book examines *how* Luther put his evangelical theology to work in actual cases of pastoral care.

A primary window into Luther's pastoral care is provided in his letters. If his open letters, theological opinion pieces, and dedicatory epistles are included, Luther's correspondence totals around three thousand known pieces (Tappert, p. 22).[3] From these extant letters, Theodore Tappert has helpfully provided a topical sampling under the title of his classic anthology, *Luther: Letters of Spiritual Counsel.* This volume makes significant Luther texts available for investigation, and they yield rich glimpses into how Luther applied evangelical doctrine to a variety of spiritual crises ranging from troubled marriages to comfort for the grieving, from doubt and despondence to afflictions faced by the imprisoned. *Martin Luther: Preacher of the Cross* relies on these sources.

Pastoral Theology: The Art of Making Distinctions

For Luther, genuine pastoral care could be nothing other than a theological undertaking. That is, it had to do not with finding a solution psychologically or socially, but with God addressing the human being in Law and Gospel, in wrath and grace, in condemnation and consolation. Luther puts it most pointedly in his lectures on Psalm 51 where he observes that "the sinful man is one who is oppressed by his conscience and tossed

1 For example, see Thomas Oden, *Care of Souls in the Classical Tradition* (Philadelphia: Fortress Press, 1984) and Andrew Purves, *Pastoral Theology in the Classical Tradition* (Louisville: Westminster/John Knox Press, 2001). One might also see Leonard M. Hummel, *Clothed in Nothingness: Consolation for Suffering* (Minneapolis: Fortress Press, 2003). Hummel seeks to restore the Lutheran tradition for pastoral care but works largely from the perspective of the social sciences, and his theological orientation seems heavily weighted in a more existentialist approach.

2 See, for example, Helmut Lieberg, *Amt und Ordination bei Luther und Melanchthon* (Göttingen: Vandenhoeck & Ruprecht, 1962) and Robert Kolb, "Ministry in Martin Luther and the Lutheran Confessions" in *Called and Ordained: Lutheran Perspectives on the Office of the Ministry,* ed. Todd Nichol and Marc Kolden (Minneapolis: Fortress Press, 1990), 49–66.

3 The unsurpassed study of Luther's pastoral care literature remains Gerhard Ebeling, *Luthers Seelsorge: Theologie in der Vielfalt der Lebenssituationen an seinen Briefen dargestellt* (Tübingen: J. C. B. Mohr, 1997).

to and fro, not knowing where to turn. Therefore we are not dealing here with a philosophical knowledge of man, which defines man as a rational animal and so forth. Such things are for science to discuss, not theology. So a lawyer speaks of man as an owner and master of property, and a physician speaks of man as healthy or sick. But a theologian discusses man as a sinner" (AE 12:310). So, for Luther, theology has a very specific task. "The proper subject of theology is man guilty of sin and condemned, and God the Justifier and Savior of man the sinner. Whatever is asked or discussed in theology outside this subject, is error and poison" (AE 12:311). Pastoral care concerns itself with this "proper subject" as the pastor must know how to distinguish the Law from the Gospel so that the sinner is identified as guilty and God is demonstrated to be gracious to the sinner for the sake of Christ.

Luther's pastoral theology is the exercise of this necessary distinction. "Such a proper distinction between the function of the Law and that of the Gospel keeps all genuine theology in its correct use. It also establishes us believers in a position as judges over all styles of life and over all the dogmas of men. Finally, it provides us with a faculty for testing all the spirits (1 John 4:1). By contrast, because the papists have completely intermingled and confused the doctrine of the Law and that of the Gospel, they have been unable to teach anything certain either about faith or about works or about styles of life or about judging the spirits. And the same thing is happening to the sectarians today" (AE 26:331).[4] For Luther, the distinction between the Law and the Gospel is not a theoretical identification of specific texts as either Law or Gospel; it is instead a functional distinction that is critical for pastoral diagnosis of a person's spiritual condition before God. Without this distinction, one cannot "test the spirits," that is, discern the truth of Christ from human fabrications or demonic counterfeits. The distinction of the Law from the Gospel not only preserves the integrity of theology, but it also enables the pastor to use this theology evangelically so that the guilty are broken by the Law and those so crushed are vivified by the word of forgiveness to live under and in the righteousness of Christ.

This functional distinction between the Law and the Gospel is not self-taught. The pastor must always be under the tutelage of the Holy Spirit if he is to acquire the capacity to rightly handle God's Law and Gospel. Luther aptly expresses this in a Table Talk of 1531: "There's no man living on earth who knows how to distinguish between the law and the gospel.

4 See the helpful overview of Luther's teaching on Law and Gospel by Hans Joachim Iwand, *The Righteousness of Faith According to Luther*, trans. Randi H. Lundell (Eugene, OR: Wipf and Stock Publishers, 2008), 39–56.

We may think we understand it when we are listening to a sermon, but we're far from it. Only the Holy Spirit knows this. Even the man Christ was so wanting in understanding when he was in the vineyard that an angel from heaven had to console him [John 12:27–29]; though he was a doctor from heaven he was strengthened by the angel. Because I've been writing so much and so long about it, you'd think I'd know the distinction, but when a crisis comes I recognize very well that I am far, far from understanding. So God alone should and must be our holy master" (AE 54:127). Correctly distinguishing the Law from the Gospel is an elusive task for pastors. The human conscience is given to vacillate, often unpredictably, between excuse making and self-accusation, between denial and despair. Luther recognized how difficult it is for a pastor in the thick of a crisis to know how and when to speak the Law, whose job it is always to accuse, and the Gospel, which can only be heard as good and liberating news by those who are already broken by their sin.

The office of the Law is to kill; it cannot do otherwise. Luther says "the function of the Law is only to kill, yet in such a way that God may be able to make alive. Thus the Law was not given merely for the sake of death; but because man is proud and supposes that he is wise, righteous, and holy, therefore it is necessary that he be humbled by the Law, in order that this beast, the presumption of righteousness, may be killed, since man cannot live unless it is killed" (AE 26:335). It is only when the Law has done its convicting and damning work, seeking out the sinner, stripping him of every excuse, and consigning him to death, that the Gospel can be heard in its promissory fullness. The Law always finds the sinner; the Gospel creates the saint by a word that gives and bestows life to the dead. Only where the Law has done its work will the Gospel be heard. While the Law announces and delivers condemnation, the Gospel announces and delivers Christ Jesus for the forgiveness of sins for "it is the proper function of Christ alone to justify the sinner" (AE 26:259).

In a letter to Joachim Mörlin of Göttingen in October 1544, Luther encourages this zealous pastor in the preaching task: "Do you not have the Law and the Gospel? According to these the Word of God must be rightly divided in order that you may wound and heal, kill and make alive. Perhaps you hope in vain that all will hear and love the Word, or perhaps you center attention on the Law to the exclusion of the Gospel, so that the people think they are listening to you instead of God or feel that they are being subjected to compulsion" (Tappert, p. 310). Luther reminds Mörlin that he should not want to be more successful than Elijah or Christ Himself. Luther cautions the pastor about his eagerness to be a faithful preacher: "Be gentle with those who are gentle, and let those who resist your preaching of the Law quarrel with God about it, just so that you have done your duty" (Tappert, p. 311).

Making Pastors the Lutheran Way: *Oratio, Meditatio, Tentatio*

Luther describes the making of theologians who can distinguish the Law from the Gospel in his 1539 *Preface to the Wittenberg Edition of Luther's German Writings* using three Latin terms: *oratio, meditatio,* and *tentatio.* The popular medieval scheme for theology was *lectio, oratio, contemplatio.* Luther breaks from this pattern. Westhelle observes "Luther's schema begins with *oratio,* which is more than prayer; it is all God-talk, talk of and to God when one knows that reason will not suffice. Second is *meditatio*—in which he includes *lectio*—which is not limited to meditation in the internal sense but also 'external,' hence engaging others in reflection. Luther does not follow the third medieval rule, *contemplatio,* but instead he brings up a very different and original concept, *tentatio,* which becomes the foremost—the 'touchstone' he calls it—and the last characteristic of theological reflection."[5] Thus Luther moves away from the speculative theology of scholasticism and the contemplative spirituality of mysticism.

Luther used three Latin words to describe how theologians are made: *oratio, meditatio, tentatio.* **Oratio** is most often translated as "prayer," but for Luther this definition needs to be nuanced to make it clear that genuine prayer grows out of God's Word addressed to us. We speak to God in prayer because He has first spoken to us in His Gospel. In this sense, then, *oratio* would have to do both with proclamation and prayer. **Meditatio** is the root of the English word "meditation." Unlike contemporary spiritual practices often derived from oriental religions, Luther's notion of meditation was not introspective or mystical but an engagement with God's Word that is heard with ear and pondered in the heart. For Luther, meditation carries with it imagery that is visceral—consuming and digesting the Word of the Lord so that its energies are imparted to the believer to fortify faith and bear fruit in vocation. Finally, **tentatio** is understood by Luther as a spiritual testing and affliction that God uses to drive the Christian to reliance in Christ alone. *Oratio* leads to *meditatio,* and *meditatio* to *tentatio.* The reverse is also true; for in spiritual testing

5 Vitor Westhelle, *The Scandalous Cross* (Minneapolis: Fortress Press, 2006), 35–36. Also see John Kleinig, "*Oratio, Meditatio, Tentatio*: What Makes a Theologian?" *Concordia Theological Quarterly* (July 2002): 255–67.

and affliction, the Christian is driven to ponder more deeply the promises of God and such meditation opens the lips to call upon the name of the Lord in confession and prayer.

For Luther "Holy Scriptures constitute a book which turns the wisdom of all other books into foolishness, because not one teaches about eternal life except this one alone" (AE 34:285). *Oratio* is anchored in the reading and hearing of these Scriptures that create faith in Christ Jesus and kindle prayer. This is the prayer that is modeled by David in Psalm 119: " 'Teach me, Lord, Lord instruct me, lead me, show me' [Psalm 119:26 et al]. . . . Although he well knew and daily heard and read the text of Moses and other books besides, still he wants to lay hold of the real teacher of the Scriptures himself, so he may not seize upon them pell-mell with his reason and become his own teacher. For such practice gives rise to factious spirits who allow themselves to nurture the delusion that the Scriptures are subject to them and can be easily grasped with their reason, as if they were *Markolf* or Aesop's Fables, for which no Holy Spirit and no prayers are needed" (AE 34:286). Oswald Bayer, a contemporary Luther scholar, comments, "Almost from the outset, Psalm 119 takes on fundamental significance for Luther's battle with the pope, who wants to prevent him from remaining with the word through which 'I became a Christian': the word of absolution. From the beginning of the Reformation, this psalm is seen as a prayer for the victory of God's word against its enemies. In fact, it is seen as a double prayer that was turned into a hymn verse in 1543: Lord, keep us steadfast in your word and curb the pope's and the Turk's sword."[6]

The Word of God is heard with the ear engaging the heart and the mind of those who receive it in faith. With the lips, this implanted Word is confessed, proclaimed, and prayed. *Oratio* leads to *meditatio* or meditation on the Word of God. For Luther this meditation is not an exercise of spirituality that turns the believer inward in silent reflection. *Meditatio* is grounded in the external word (*externum verbum*) to use the language of the Smalcald Articles (K-W, p. 322). For Luther, the *meditatio* is oral and outward. So in his Genesis lectures he states, "Let him who wants to contemplate in the right way reflect on his Baptism; let him read his Bible, hear sermons, honor father and mother, and come to the aid of a brother in distress. But let him not shut himself up in a nook . . . and there entertain himself with his devotions and thus suppose that he is sitting in God's

6 Oswald Bayer, *Theology the Lutheran Way*, trans. Jeffrey G. Silcock and Mark C. Mattes (Grand Rapids: Eerdmans, 2007), 40.

bosom and has fellowship with God without Christ, without the Word, without the sacraments" (AE 3:275).

Evangelical meditation draws one outside of himself into the promises of Christ (faith) and into the need of the neighbor (love). Thus Luther is dead set against any and all forms of enthusiasm[7] that would rely on visions or miraculous appearances:

> Christ once appeared visible here on earth, and showed his glory, and according to the divine purpose of God finished the work of redemption and deliverance of mankind. I do not desire he should come to me once more in the same manner, neither would I should he send an angel unto me. Nay, though an angel should appear before mine eyes from heaven, yet it would not add to my belief; for I have of my Saviour Christ Jesus bond and seal; I have his Word, Spirit, and sacrament; thereon I depend, and desire no new revelations. And the more steadfastly to confirm me in this resolution, to hold solely to God's Word, and not to give credit to any visions or revelations, I shall relate the following circumstance: —On Good Friday last, I being in my chamber in fervent prayer, contemplating with myself, how Christ my Saviour on the cross suffered and died for our sins, there suddenly appeared on the wall a bright vision of our Saviour Christ, with the five wounds, steadfastly looking upon me, as if it had been Christ himself corporeally. At first sight, I thought it had been some celestial revelation, but I reflected that it must needs be an illusion and juggling of the devil, for Christ appeared to us in his Word, and in a meaner and more humble form; therefore I spake to the vision thus: Avoid thee, confounded devil: I know no other Christ than he who was crucified, and who in his Word is pictured and presented unto me. Whereupon the image vanished, clearly showing of whom it came.[8]

7 See Bayer, *Theology the Lutheran Way,* 40. Here Bayer quotes a Luther sermon on Genesis 28 of December 1520: "If they bore their way into heaven with their heads and look around they will find no one, because Christ lies in a crib and in a woman's lap. So let them fall back down again and break their necks." Bayer also writes, "Those who want to search for the Holy Spirit deep inside themselves, in a realm too deep for words to express, will find only ghosts, not God" (55).

8 Cited in H. T. Kerr, *A Compend of Luther's Theology* (Philadelphia: Westminster Press, 1943), 57.

Meditation is immersion into the text of Holy Scripture. It is the ongoing hearing of God's Word read and preached so that the one who hears Christ is enlivened to trust His promises and, in his calling in the world, is equipped to respond to the needs of the neighbor. Luther likened meditation to a cow chewing its cud. In his commentary on Deuteronomy 14:1 of 1525, he writes: "To chew the cud, however, is to take up the Word with delight and meditate with supreme diligence, so that (according to the proverb) one does not permit it to go into one ear and out the other, but holds it firmly in the heart, swallows it, and absorbs it into the intestines" (AE 9:136).

Luther provides a practical tool for such meditation in his celebrated devotional booklet *A Simple Way to Pray* written for the Wittenberg barber Peter Beskendorf in 1535 where Luther suggests that a person meditate on each of the commandments of the Decalogue "in their fourfold aspect, namely, as a school text, song book, penitential book, and prayer book" (AE 43:189).[9] Luther encourages his barber to dwell on the text—to engage the didactic, doxological, diagnostic, and intercessory dimensions of the text. Those who stand in front of the text are taught, brought to praise God, have their sins uncovered, and are given material for their prayer.

While Luther prepared this tract for a layman, it certainly applies to the pastor whose life is given to the service of the text of Holy Scripture for the sake of proclamation and pastoral care. The Psalms, in Luther's estimation, were an especially fertile place for preachers to meditate. In his lectures on Psalm 1 (1519–1521), he states "Therefore it is the office of a man whose proper duty it is to converse on something, to discourse on the Law of the Lord. . . . For this meditation consists first in close attention to the words of the Law, and then drawing together the various parts of Scripture. And this is a pleasant hunt, a game rather like the play of the stags in the forest [Ps. 29:2]. . . . For out of this will proceed a sermon to the people which is well informed in the Law of the Lord" (AE 14:296). The preacher is not meditating on the Word simply for his own spiritual well-being but for those placed under his curacy in the church. He meditates on the Word that he may have something to say from the Lord to the people he is given to serve.

For Luther, meditation does not take place in a spiritual vacuum, in isolation from the temptations of the world, the flesh, and the devil. God

9 AE 43:189. Also note Brecht's observation: "Nowhere is the connection between order and freedom in Luther's practice of prayer so clearly seen as in his advice for Master Peter." Martin Brecht, *Martin Luther: The Preservation of the Church 1532–1546*, trans. James L. Schaaf (Minneapolis: Fortress Press, 1993), 14.

uses *tentatio* (spiritual affliction, trial, and temptation) to drive away from self and to His promises alone. Bayer captures Luther's thought: "Anyone who meditates can expect to suffer. Luther once again also allows Psalm 119 to prescribe this experience. Therefore in light of this third rule, he expects students of theology also to see themselves in the role of the psalmist who 'complains so often about all kinds of enemies . . . that he has to put up with because he meditates, that is, because he is occupied with God's word (as has been said) in all manner of ways.' "[10]

Tentatio is no stranger to those who serve in the pastoral office. Luther understands this *tentatio* as a spiritual affliction that drives faithful servants to rely on the sure and certain promises of Christ alone. Luther comments on Genesis 32:32 saying, "Our Lord Jesus Christ, tested Jacob not to destroy him but to confirm and strengthen him and that in his fight he might more correctly learn the might of the promise" (AE 5:144).[11] God does His work under opposites: "When God works, He turns His face away at first and seems to be the devil, not God" (AE 7:103).

Temptation, which is entailed in the *tentatio*, is necessary for the Christian life in general but especially for preachers of the Word. "I did not learn my theology all at once, but had to search constantly deeper and deeper for it. My temptations did that for me, for no one can understand Holy Scripture without practice and temptations. That is what the enthusiasts and sects lack. They don't have the right critic, the devil, who is the best teacher of theology. If we don't have that kind of devil, then we become nothing but speculative theologians, who do nothing but walk around in our own thoughts and speculate with our reason alone as to whether things should be like this, or like that," says Luther in a Table Talk of 1532 (AE 54:50).

The experience of temptation prepares and equips the pastor to serve as an "instructor of consciences" by granting him the capacity to distinguish the Law from the Gospel, directing the afflicted away from the erratic and errant movement of the conscience from excuse-making to accusation. A conscience ceases to rationalize sin or be terrorized by the Law only when it rests in the forgiveness of sins. "Therefore I admonish you, especially those of you who are to become instructors of consciences, as well as each of you individually, that you exercise yourselves continually by study, by reading, by meditation and by prayer, so that in temptation you will be

10 Bayer, *Theology the Lutheran Way*, 60.

11 Here see Mary Jane Haemig, "Prayer as Talking Back to God," *Lutheran Quarterly* (Autumn 2009): 270–95.

able to instruct consciences, both your own and others, and take them from the law to grace, from active righteous to passive righteousness, in short from Moses to Christ. In affliction and in the conflict of conscience it is the devil's habit to frighten us with the law and to set against us the consciousness of sin, our wicked past, the wrath and judgment of God, hell, and eternal death, so that he may drive us into despair, subject us to himself, and pluck us from Christ" (AE 26:10).

Like the apostle Paul in 2 Corinthians 1:3–4, who speaks of the comfort we give to others in their afflictions as flowing from the comfort we have received from Christ, Luther speaks out of the *tentatio* that he had experienced. No doubt that the judgment of Walther von Loewenich is on target: "The secret of Luther's proficiency in pastoral care was that he himself had known what it was like to experience attacks of despair [*Anfechtung*]."[12]

Luther's triad, *oratio, meditatio,* and *tentatio,* shapes the ongoing life of the pastor as he is forever dependent on the power of God's promises. The crosses and afflictions of the pastoral life drive the pastor to meditate on the words of the Lord, and God's Word opens his lips for confession, prayer, praise, and proclamation with confidence that the divine Word accomplishes God's purposes and does not return to Him empty.

Pastoral Theology as Theology of the Cross

Luther's pastoral theology is the theology of the cross in contrast to sundry theologies of glory that dominated the religious landscape of the sixteenth century and continue to dominate the twenty-first century. Although Luther's use of the exact terminology "theology of the cross" is limited, the approach expressed in the term permeates Luther's thinking. Commenting on 1 John in 1527, the reformer notes "My work has only one purpose: to keep you in the doctrine handed down previously. It is my desire to keep you in simplicity against the new teachers. Remain in simplicity and in the old doctrine you have received. Above all, beware of the boasting, of seeking glory. In the Holy Scriptures the desire to boast is a temptation of the devil. Therefore God has ordered things in such a way that the Word of the Gospel should be the Word of the cross. It is His purpose to suppress that empty glory" (AE 30:240–41).

---

12 Walther von Loewenich, *Martin Luther: The Man and His Work,* trans. Lawrence Denef (Minneapolis: Augsburg Publishing House, 1982), 359–360. Also see Lennart Pinomaa, "The Problem of Affliction" in *Faith Victorious: An Introduction to Luther's Theology,* trans. Walter J. Kukkonen (Philadelphia: Fortress Press, 1963), 89–100, and Mark D. Thompson, "Luther on Despair," in *The Consolations of Theology,* ed. Brian S. Rosner (Grand Rapids: Eerdmans, 2008), 51–74.

In a similar way, Luther expresses the theology of the cross (*theologia crucis*) in his 1521 commentary on the *Magnificat* where he writes of God's twofold work, describing it in terms of the Law and the Gospel, the scattering of the boastful and the exaltation of the lowly who trust in Him. This work of God, Luther says, "is done quietly and in secret, and no one knows of it until it is all accomplished; so that this power, or arm, can be understood only by faith" (AE 21:339). Suffering is not a sign that God has forsaken the faithful, and outward prosperity is not to be confused with divine endorsement. Noting the way God works in apparent weakness, Luther says, "He lets the godly become powerless and to be brought low, until everyone supposes their end is near, whereas in these very things He is present to them with all His power, yet so hidden and secret that even those who suffer oppression do not feel it but only believe. There is the fullness of God's power and His outstretched arm. For where man's strength ends, God's strength begins, begins provided that faith is present and waits on Him. And when the oppression comes to an end, it becomes manifest what great strength was hidden underneath the weakness. Even Christ was powerless on the cross; and yet there He performed His mightiest work and conquered sin, death, hell, devil, and all evil" (AE 21:340).

The theology of the cross gives focus and direction to his preaching and his care of souls for it centers not in human wisdom that seeks to attain righteousness through obedience to the Law, the exercise of the will which is presumed to be free, or the application of the principles of reason. By way of contrast, Luther asserts that saving righteousness is found only through faith in the crucified Messiah. This is the wisdom of the cross, which interprets all of life for the believer.[13] Hermann Sasse captures this essential aspect of Luther's theology of the cross: "Obviously the 'theology of the cross' does not mean that for a theologian the church year shrinks together into nothing but Good Friday. Rather it means that Christmas, Easter, and Pentecost cannot be understood without Good Friday. Next to Irenaeus and Athanasius, Luther was the greatest theologian of the incarnation. He was this because in the background of the manger he saw the cross. His understanding of the Easter victory was equal to that of any theologian of the Eastern Church. He understood it because he understood the victory of the Crucified One. The same can be said of his understanding of the work

13 Here see Regin Prenter, *Luther's Theology of the Cross* (Philadelphia: Fortress Press, 1971). Prenter writes, "Already in his earlier thought, Luther regarded the theology of the cross not merely as one part of theology but as theology in its totality, that is, theology in so far as it is at all capable of understanding the unity underlying the antitheses in the divine works: God's righteousness under his judgment, his grace under his anger, the life which he bestows even in the midst of death, his power to turn the present evil into a thing of good" (2).

of the Holy Spirit. Always it is from the cross that everything is understood, because hidden in the cross is the deepest essence of God's revelation. Because this is so, Luther's *theologia crucis* (theology of the cross) wants to be more than just one of many theological theories that have appeared in Christian history. It stands against its opposite, the prevailing theology in Christendom, the *theologia gloriae* (theology of glory) as Luther calls it, and claims to be that right and Scriptural theology with which the church of Christ stands or falls. Only of the preaching of this theology, Luther maintains, can it be said that it is the preaching of the Gospel."[14]

For Luther, the theology of the cross signals the fact that God comes to humanity in the baby of Bethlehem and the man of Calvary, Jesus Christ. It is in this sense, to use the language of Lowell Green, a "theology from below."[15] Pastoral care is not a technique to move people toward a relationship with God based on the Law, the will, or reason. Instead evangelical pastoral care is God's movement to sinners in Christ. It is God drawing near to those who cannot rescue themselves as He comes to us in the means He has appointed—Baptism, preaching, Absolution, and the Lord's Supper. For Luther, pastoral care is always preaching or proclamation in the broadest sense of the term, for it has to do with the delivery of the divine promise in the scriptural Word, the preached Word, and the sacramental Word.

The theology of the cross will not permit the preaching of the cross to become preaching *about* the cross. Note Luther's words in his treatise, *A Meditation on Christ's Passion* (1519): "Some people meditate on Christ's passion by venting their anger on the Jews. This singing and ranting about wretched Judas satisfies them, for they are in the habit of complaining about other people, of condemning and reproaching their adversaries. That might well be a meditation on the wickedness of Judas and the Jews, but not on the sufferings of Christ. . . . Some feel pity for Christ, lamenting and bewailing his innocence. They are like the women who followed Christ from Jerusalem and were chided and told by Christ that it would be better to weep for themselves and their children (Luke 23:27–28). . . . They contemplate Christ's passion aright who view it with a terror-stricken

---

14 Hermann Sasse, "The Theology of the Cross" in *We Confess Jesus Christ*, trans. and ed. Norman E. Nagel (St. Louis: Concordia, 1984), 39. Also note Walter Künneth on the significance of this theology of the cross: "Thus linking up with Paul, and not least looking back to Luther, the *theologia crucis* is perceived to be the heart of the evangelical doctrine of salvation." Walther Künneth, *The Theology of the Resurrection*, trans. James W. Leitch (St. Louis: Concordia, 1965), 150.

15 See Lowell C. Green, "Martin Luther on Coming to God from 'Below' in Its Implications for the Church Today" in *A Reader in Pastoral Theology*, ed. John T. Pless (Fort Wayne: Concordia Theological Seminary Press, 2002), 42–45.

heart and a despairing conscience" (AE 42:7–8). Then Luther goes on to say "You cast your sins from yourself and onto Christ when you firmly believe that his wounds and sufferings are your sins, to be borne and paid for by him, as we read in Isaiah 53:6, 'The Lord has laid on him the iniquity of us all.' St. Peter says, 'in his body has he borne our sins on the wood of the cross' (1 Peter 2:24). St. Paul says, 'God has made him a sinner for us, so that through him we would be made just' (1 Cor. 5:21). You must stake everything on these and similar verses" (AE 42:12). Preaching about the cross would be descriptive discourse on the events of Good Friday, but to preach the cross is to set forth the crucified Christ as God for you so that the hearer knows that Jesus' Passion is God's own remedy for the conscience infected and tormented by sin. The preaching of the cross calls forth faith, trust in the divine promise that in Christ God Himself is for sinners and not against them.

The Means of Pastoral Care

Walter von Loewenich's assessment gets to the heart of the matter. "The theology of the cross is theology of faith."[16] That is to say, faith receives and lays hold of all that God gives us in His crucified Son, who alone is our righteousness and life. Luther understands the work of pastoral care to be directed by the word of the cross delivered in sermon and sacrament so that living faith in Christ might be created and sustained. The confession of the Third Article of the Apostles' Creed in the Small Catechism, "I believe that I cannot by my own reason or strength believe in Jesus Christ, my Lord, or come to Him, but the Holy Spirit has called me by the Gospel, enlightened me with His gifts, sanctified and kept me in the true faith," is not limited to a description of the Spirit's work in conversion. This is an ongoing reality for the believer. Without the word of the cross continually in the ears and heart of the believer, faith withers. Pastors must preach and teach the one true faith, speak the absolution recalling sinners to their Baptism in repentance, and distribute the testament of Christ's body and blood for the forgiveness of sins.

In a sermon preached Easter Tuesday of 1529 on John 20:19–23, Luther proclaims, "After He has strengthened them in faith in His resurrection through His Word and work, He commits the office of preaching to them and gives them power and authority to remit and retain sins. In this way He indicates what the office of preaching is, namely an office on which our

16 Walther von Loewenich, *Luther's Theology of the Cross,* trans. Herbert J. A. Bouman (Minneapolis: Augsburg Publishing House, 1976), 21.

life and salvation depend. Through His mouth He brings us the Word. He commits the Word to human beings. The Word, even though it is preached through human beings, brings life and salvation. It is a remarkable office and Word that He commits to the disciples, and for this reason it should be highly esteemed. St. Paul praises the Word of forgiveness of sins in all his Epistles. For him the office of preaching is so precious that he calls it the 'Word of reconciliation with God' and 'a proclamation' in the stead of Christ (2 Cor. 5[:19–20]), 'a ministry' of the Spirit (2 Cor. 3[:8])" (AE 69:352–53).[17] Preaching is the delivery of Christ's forgiveness to sinners. In this sense, preaching extends beyond the pulpit and embraces all that the pastor does as he administers the Gospel in the various occasions of human life both corporately and individually.

The sermon and the Sacrament stand together in Luther. The forgiveness of sins lies at the heart of the Sacrament. He drives this home with the triple repletion of "given for you" and "shed for the forgiveness of sins" in the Sixth Chief Part of the Small Catechism. Oswald Bayer observes: "Luther does not concentrate on the threefold repetition of the two phrases 'given for you' and 'shed for the forgiveness of sins' just by chance. God's turning toward the sinner, the promise that creates faith, empowered by the death and resurrection of Jesus Christ, cannot be summarized any more succinctly and specifically than by using these words. This must be stated clearly as a critique of the depersonalizing speech about the 'bread of life' or the diminution of the Lord's Supper to become a generic lovefest. The Lord's Supper is not some diffuse celebration of life but is defined in a precise way in its essence by means of the connection between the Word of Christ that has effective power and the faith."[18]

The forgiveness won on the cross is delivered in the Supper. "Therefore it is absurd for them to say that Christ's body and blood are not given and poured out for us in the Lord's Supper and hence that we cannot have forgiveness of sins in the sacrament. Although the work took place on the cross and forgiveness of sins has been acquired, yet it cannot come to us in any other way than through the Word" (LC V 31; K-W, p. 469). Thus Luther urges believers who are haunted by their sins and hounded by the devil

---

17 On Luther's understanding of preaching, see Oswald Bayer, "Preaching the Word," *Lutheran Quarterly* (Autumn 2009): 249–69; Fred Meuser, *Luther the Preacher* (Minneapolis: Augsburg, 1983); John T. Pless, "Martin Luther: Preacher of the Cross," *Concordia Theological Quarterly* (April–July 1987): 83–101; and H. S. Wilson, "Luther on Preaching" in *The Pastoral Luther: Essays on Martin Luther's Practical Theology*, ed. Timothy J. Wengert (Grand Rapids: Eerdmans, 2009), 100–114.

18 Oswald Bayer, *Martin Luther's Theology: A Contemporary Interpretation*, trans. Thomas Trapp (Grand Rapids: Eerdmans, 2008), 272.

to go to the Supper to receive the testament of Christ's atoning work—the forgiveness of sins.

Along with preaching and the Lord's Supper, Luther prizes Confession and Absolution as a means of pastoral care. The focus in Confession and Absolution is not on the confession per se, but on the absolution. Disconnected from the absolution, confession turns into just another effort to save ourselves. Then the old Adam begins to reckon that he is right with God because his confession was completely sincere or deeply heartfelt. Or he reckons that he has been pious and courageous by making individual confession a part of his regular spiritual discipline. In the Medieval Church, the requirement of no less than an annual trip to the confessional booth and the enumeration of specific sins had transformed confession into a spiritual torture chamber rather than an occasion for broken bones to be made glad in the word from the Lord: "I forgive you all your sins." It is at this point that Luther filters the old practice of private confession through the sieve of the Gospel so that it could be reclaimed for the sake of terrified consciences. Thus Luther develops five major points in his "A Brief Exhortation to Confession" included in the Large Catechism:

> Confession should be voluntary and free of papal tyranny.
>
> The practice of confession ought to be free of the unreasonable and tortuous demand that the penitent be able to enumerate his sins.
>
> People should be taught how to use confession evangelically for the comfort of terrified consciences.
>
> Christian liberty ought not be used as an excuse for setting private confession aside.
>
> Private confession stands with other forms of confession in the church (Fifth Petition of the Lord's Prayer where we confess to God and the neighbor). (LC "A Brief Exhortation to Confession"; K-W, pp. 476–80).

These pastoral themes are reflected in Luther's short order of confession included in the Small Catechism (SC IV 15–29; K-W, pp. 360–62). The insertion of a short order of confession between Holy Baptism and the Sacrament of the Altar was intended by Luther to catechize people in the evangelical use of confession and absolution. "Luther's discussion of confession, along with the shape of his liturgical rite, shows how he redefines its essence and practice so that it ceases to be a burden and instead becomes an instrument by which the Gospel is conveyed personally to an individual."[19]

Luther's approach to pastoral care centers in the preaching of the cross and the administration of the sacraments for the comfort of terrified consciences and the strengthening of faith to live under the cross in the lively hope of the resurrection. Grounded in God's Word and Sacraments, the work of the pastor in caring for the flock includes admonition, consolation, and support in life and in death.[20]

---

19 Charles Arand, *That I May Be His Own: An Overview of Luther's Catechisms* (St. Louis: Concordia, 2000), 169.

20 Here see Reinhard Slenczka, "Luther's Care of Souls for Our Times," *Concordia Theological Quarterly* (January 2003): 33–63.

CHAPTER 1

The Visitation and the Catechisms: Diagnosis and Remedy

> May God, the Father of all mercy, grant us through Jesus Christ, his dear Son, the spirit of unity and the power to do his will. Even though the finest spirit of unity prevails among us we still have our hands full to do good and be established by the power of God. What would happen if there were disunity and disagreement among us? The devil has become neither pious nor devout this year, nor will he ever be so. So let us be on guard and anxious to keep (as Paul teaches) the spiritual unity in the bond of love and peace [Eph. 4:3]. Amen. (AE 40:273)

Visitation: A Catholic Practice

The practice of visitation might be said to reach back to the New Testament Church where after the Jerusalem Council Paul says to Barnabas, "Let us return and visit the brothers in every city where we proclaimed the word of the Lord, and see how they are doing" (Acts 15:36). The term "visitation" became prominent in the ninth century, but the practice goes back earlier into the fifth century where bishops were expected to make official visits to examine, inspect, teach, and, if necessary, correct errant practices in parish life. A model for such visitation can be found in the tenth century in a handbook prepared by the abbot of Regino of Prüm written at the directive of the Archbishop of Trier, which included an inventory of ninety-six items of inquiry centering on conditions of parochial life, the integrity of clerical life, and pastoral care.

By the late Middle Ages, the practice of visitation had gradually declined. Early in the fifteenth century, Jean Gerson delivered a passionate plea for churchly reform including a scheme for the visitation of parishes. "Thus, while sixteenth-century reformers claimed in their pronouncements to have revived a long-defunct ancient practice, they could, in fact, build their own visitation procedures on tried and established precedents."[1]

A Reformation Effort

On June 24, 1524, Elector John the Steadfast (1468–1532) wrote to Luther suggesting a visitation: "May God hear our complaint, but there are too many enthusiasts, and these are causing us plenty of trouble up here. But in my opinion there would be no better way of quieting things down than for you to take some time to travel from one town to another in this principality and to see for yourself (as Paul did) what kinds of preachers are serving the faithful in the towns. I believe that among us here in Thuringia you could hardly do a more Christian task. Whichever preachers proved unsuited you could then remove with the help of the authorities."[2] An early attempt at a visitation was made just after the beginning of the year in 1525 when Elector John commissioned Jacob Strauss, the pastor in Eisenach, and ducal councilman Burkhard Hund of Wendheim to visit the congregations in and around Eisenach. Hund was unable to participate in the visitation leaving Strauss on his own. The first effort proved futile. A second attempt was made in March of the same year with the visitor provided with documentation authorizing the work. Pastor Nicholas Hausmann in Zwickau undertook another visitation on May 2, 1525.

Since he believed that poor ecclesiastical supervision had been responsible for the growth of abuses in the pre-Reformation church, Luther recognized a need for evangelical oversight exercised through visitation. Worried about the chaotic conditions in the Saxon congregations, Luther urged the Elector John to take measures to ensure stability and good order in the religious and social life of his territory.[3] In 1527, John issued *Instructions and Order for Dispatching Visitors*, a catalog of items to be investigated by teams of four appointed visitors. Yet this document proved insufficient for the task.

---

1 Gerald Strauss, "Visitations" in *The Oxford Encyclopedia of the Reformation*, vol. 4, ed. Hans Hillerbrand (Oxford: Oxford University Press, 1996), 238.

2 Cited from WA BR 3:310/44ff in Heinrich Bornkamm, *Luther in Mid-Career 1521–1530*, trans. E. Theodore Bachmann (Philadelphia: Fortress Press, 1983), 485.

3 "Luther took the momentous step and—so he himself, at any rate, viewed it—told the princes that 'out of Christian love' he wanted certain persons appointed as visitors. He derives the office of the visitors from the original meaning of the term 'bishop' and 'archbishop' (WA 26, 197, 17ff). Although here, too, he considers the bishop the pastor (*Pfarrherr*), who 'should visit, look after, and supervise his parishioners' (*pfarrkinder besuchen, warten und auff sehen sol*), 'the archbishop' should 'visit, look after, and supervise such bishops to see how they are teaching.' " Werner Elert, *The Structure of Lutheranism*, trans. Walter Hansen (St. Louis: Concordia, 1962), 372.

Melanchthon then set about drafting *Instructions for the Visitors of Parish Pastors*. This document would provide a theological platform for the visitations. John Agricola (1492–1566) objected to this document, believing that Melanchthon was conceding to the Romanists.[4] In November 1527, Luther would bring Agricola and Melanchthon together to attempt to reconcile their competing positions on the relationship of repentance and faith, which was at the heart of Agricola's objection to Melanchthon's document. Further consultation and correspondence would lead to revisions and a final draft of the articles for visitation but not without questioning on a temporary allowance of communion under one kind[5] and marriage matters by the Elector.

Early in 1528, the Elector would direct Luther to prepare a preface for the *Instructions*. Luther's preface begins with the recollection of various examples of visitations in not only the New Testament but also in the Old Testament. He recalls, for example, that Peter traveled among the Jewish congregations in Acts 9 while Barnabas and Paul visited the places in which they had preached in Acts 5. He notes that when the apostles heard of how the Word of the Lord was received in Samaria, Peter and John were dispatched there. Luther sees examples of visitation in the Old Testament in the narratives of Samuel's travels to Ramah, Nob, and Gigal. Above all, Luther observes that Christ Jesus is the visitor *par excellence*: "More than any Christ has done this kind of work on behalf of all, and on this account possessed no place on earth where he could lay his head or which he could call his own. This began even while he was in the womb, for he went with his mother over the hills to visit St. John (Luke 1:39)" (AE 40:269).

The ancient fathers, Luther observed, also practiced visitation. In fact, Luther argues that the essence of the episcopal office is to visit and examine. To be a bishop is to be a supervisor or visitor. Archbishops supervise bishops. Bishops oversee the work of parish pastors. Yet Luther argues the office fell into abuse and misuse. Luther writes, "The holy synods were forgotten. In brief that is what befell so worthy an office and nothing remained of it except the burdening and banning of people because of money, debts, and temporal goods and the making of a divine order out of

4 For a detailed treatment of the controversy with Agricola in the formation of the *Instructions*, see Martin Brecht, *Martin Luther: Shaping and Defining the Reformation 1521–1530*, trans. James L. Schaaf (Minneapolis: Fortress Press, 1990), 264ff. Agricola would argue that repentance is the consequence of the preaching of the Gospel, thus dispensing with the realities of the Law, wrath, and judgment of God. Also see Charles P. Arand, Robert Kolb, and James A. Nestingen, *The Lutheran Confessions: History and Theology of The Book of Concord* (Minneapolis: Fortress Press, 2012), 67–72.

5 The provision for communion under one kind was omitted in the second edition of the *Instructions* in 1538. See Brecht, *Martin Luther: Shaping and Defining the Reformation 1521–1532*, 266.

the bellowing of antiphons and versicles in churches. No attention is paid to how one teaches, believes, loves, how one lives a Christian life, how to care for the poor, how one comforts the weak, or punishes the unruly. They are altogether officious and gluttonous fellows who destroy what belongs to the people and do worse than nothing for them. This office has fared like all holy and ancient Christian doctrine and order—it has become the farce and contempt of the devil and Antichrist with awful and terrible destruction of souls" (AE 40:270).

Luther seeks to retrieve this venerable office from political and economic mishandling. He sees it as a pressing need that the office be restored to its pristine spiritual purpose of service to the Gospel to counteract confusion, dissension, and abuses in the evangelical parishes of Saxony. To this end, Luther commends the Elector for reconstituting the practice of visitation as the fulfillment of the office of Christian love. Because this work is undertaken and guided by "love's office," the Elector may be confident that it conforms to "God's will for the benefit of the gospel and the welfare of the wretched Christians in his territory" (AE 40:271).

By way of the preface, Luther gives his endorsement and approval to Melanchthon's *Instructions*. Observing that some had seen the *Instructions* as a recantation of evangelical teaching, Luther counters that he has carefully reviewed them and they are consistent with the aim of God's Word. Luther envisions the *Instruction*s not as a new form of the papal decree but "as a witness and confession of our faith" offered with the "hope that all devout and peaceable pastors who find their sincere joy in the gospel and delight to be of one mind with us will act as St. Paul teaches in Phil. 2[:2]. And will heed our prince and gracious lord" (AE 40:272). Luther hopes that the *Instructions* will be received in the spirit and intention in which they are offered. Congregations and pastors should willingly and peacefully receive the visitors and subject themselves in a spirit of love and humility to their work. Those who refuse are to be recognized as self-centered and undisciplined who finally separate themselves from the evangelical cause and must be recognized as "chaff on the threshing floor." Luther further adds that we "will not accommodate ourselves to them" (AE 40:273). Luther says that the Elector, even though he has no call to teach and rule in spiritual affairs, must deal with these undisciplined people just as Constantine did not tolerate the political unrest created by Arius.

The Instructions

Melanchthon includes eighteen items in the *Instructions*: The Doctrine, the Ten Commandments, True Christian Prayer, Tribulation, the Sacrament of Baptism, the Sacrament of the Altar, Christian Penance, Christian Confession, Christian Satisfaction for Sin, the Human Order of the Church, Marriage, Free Will, Christian Freedom, the Turks, Daily Worship in the Church, the Christian Ban, the Office of Superintendents, and Schools.

Melanchthon seeks to use the *Instructions* to catechize in evangelical doctrine and aims for its pastoral application in preaching and the care of souls. Thus Melanchthon begins with a discussion of the necessity that both repentance and faith be preached. Faith cannot be divorced from repentance. Without the preaching of repentance the proclamation of the forgiveness of sins will not only ring empty, it will lead to a carnal security. So evangelical preachers are to preach the Law in all of its potency so that people are brought "to repent and grieve over their sins and to fear the judgment of God" (AE 40:275). This preaching condemns gross and outward sins, but Melanchthon reminds his readers that both John the Baptist and Christ do not neglect "the greatest and most important element of repentance," namely, the condemnation of a false holiness that puts its trust in human merit or worth.

Clearly Melanchthon is addressing the antinomian teaching of Agricola when he says that some have taught repentance follows faith. The Law is preached not to make men righteous but to reveal and crush sin, and only where this takes place will the Gospel be heard as the good news that sinners are justified by faith apart from the works of the Law. The section on "the doctrine" is a brief lesson in the necessity of the right distinction of the Law from the Gospel.

The dual theme of repentance and faith is carried forward in Melanchthon's section on the Ten Commandments. Since through the Law comes knowledge of sin, the commandments are to be preached specifically to condemn various vices such as adultery, drunkenness, envy, hate, and the like. The commandments are not only to be explained. Preachers should tell their hearers how God threatens to punish sins, recalling biblical examples, so that they might learn to fear God. Such preaching is to produce repentance, that is, contrition and grief over sin and true fear of God. Melanchthon says that preachers are "to teach the people diligently that this faith [saving faith] cannot exist without earnest and true contrition and fear of God" (AE 40:276).

Melanchthon only provides explicit treatment of the First and Second Commandments in this section. He is more concerned to lay out a paradigm for teaching the commandments rather than for providing the more detailed exposition of individual commandments as Luther will come to do in the Large Catechism. Here he wishes to outline instead the threefold pattern of the Christian life: repentance, faith in the forgiveness of sins, and the doing of good works. Good works are to be done because they are pleasing to God and beneficial to the welfare of the neighbor.

The nature of the Christian's life of good works is explained in the next section under the title "True Christian Prayer." This section anticipates Luther's treatment of the Lord's Prayer in the Small Catechism even as it echoes elements from Luther's earlier sermons on prayer, for here Melanchthon accents the fact that genuine prayer is anchored in the divine commandment and promise.[6] God has commanded us to pray and has promised to hear us.

Since God has promised to hear the prayers of His people, Christians should not be frightened away from praying on account of their sins. God gives freely for Christ's sake, therefore believers are invited to make their supplications with boldness and without doubt. Christians are to be taught that God hears them for the sake of Christ and not because of formulaic repetition. Christians are to be instructed to pray for both spiritual and temporal things without setting a time or place for God's fulfillment.

Then Melanchthon picks up other aspects of the Decalogue. Christians are to be instructed in the hearing and learning of God's Word under the rubric of the Third Commandment. Obedience to parents and governing authorities is enjoined by the Fourth Commandment. Prayers are to be made for civil authorities, and taxes are to be paid. Christians are to live in such a manner "that the holy gospel is not slandered and disgraced as happens in the case of those who claim in the name of the holy gospel to be free from tithes and other temporal burdens" (AE 40:287).

The life of good works will include tribulation. Pastors need to be capable of teaching their people how to face tribulation in body and soul. Melanchthon notes that pastors should teach their people that God sends

6 See Luther's *An Exposition of the Lord's Prayer for Simple Laymen* [1519] (AE 42:15–81) and *On Rogationtide Prayer and Procession* [1519] (AE 42:83–94). In this sermon, Luther sets forth an evangelical approach to prayer that centers in God's promise and command. Recognizing the abuses that had accumulated around the blessing of the field associated with Rogate (the Fifth Sunday after Easter), Luther uses this occasion to teach that prayer is a gift of God to be exercised by faith alone. Also see Oswald Bayer, *Martin Luther's Theology: A Contemporary Interpretation*, 343–54; and Martin Lehmann, *Luther and Prayer* (Milwaukee: Northwestern Publishing House, 1985), 3–39.

tribulations to "admonish us and awaken us to patience" (AE 40:287). Christians are to be tutored to have confidence in the divine promises and call upon God in the midst of these troubles, knowing that the devil attempts to use tribulation to bring the Christian into shame and misery.

Sections follow on Baptism and the Lord's Supper. Infant Baptism is affirmed. The benefits of Baptism are to be taught so that people understand the gifts God bestows in Baptism and the value of Baptism not only as a point of initiation for children but a gift for the entire life of the Christian. Melanchthon urges the use of German in the baptismal order so that the people may understand the words and prayer. There need be no quarrel over the chrism for the real anointing is done not with oil but by the Holy Spirit.

Drawing on the Words of Institution from the Synoptic Gospels and 1 Corinthians, Melanchthon directs pastors to teach the people that the true body and blood of Christ are present in the bread and wine not by virtue of priestly power but on account of the institution of Christ. The Sacrament is not to be received as ordinary food. Pastors should teach the people to receive the Sacrament under both kinds for no one may alter the last will and testament of the Son of God.

Yet Melanchthon urges consideration of weak Christians. While the teaching of Communion under both kinds is to be taught clearly and without compromise, pastors may be allowed to commune weak believers with only the Lord's body for a time. Melanchthon notes that it would be "uncharitable" and "even un-Christian" to force these people to receive the Sacrament in both kinds or to withhold it altogether, lest they be made to sin. However such is not the case with the obstinate who know the doctrine but reject it. These are to be allowed to go their own way. This section stirred some objections from the Elector, but Luther insisted on keeping the *Instructions* in line with his principle that only the Word of God, not legislation of practice, would change spiritual conditions.

Melanchthon makes several points regarding the proper preparation for the Sacrament. First, the pastor should instruct the people as to what the Sacrament is and warn them against abusing it in a way that profanes the body and blood of the Lord (1 Corinthians 11:27). Second, the pastor should examine all communicants, inquiring of their understanding of the Sacrament. Those who show no contrition and are living in open sin are not to be admitted. Melanchthon goes on to speak of the right remembrance of Christ in the Sacrament, asserting that it is "not that the outward reception will comfort the heart, but it is a sign of the comfort and of the forgiveness of sins. This sign encourages the heart to believe that

God forgives a penitent his sins" (AE 40:293). In this way the Sacrament is to be preached. Forgiveness comes not through an outward act of eating and drinking but through faith. Melanchthon concludes this section by linking faith and love in the Sacrament. Those who partake together of the Lord's body and blood are one with each other as "one loaf" and are not to harbor envy or hate toward the fellow communicant.

Next, Melanchthon includes an article on true Christian penance, which he counts as a third sacrament.[7] Once again Melanchthon warns against a carnal or fleshly security that ignores contrition by speaking of sin in specious and generic categories. It is not simply "to know oneself" (AE 40:295). One must know one's sin. That is, one must have "contrition and sorrow over it and sincere fear of the wrath and judgment of God" (AE 40:295). Preachers must preach the Law with such incisiveness that "a person fears all his good works and understands that he sins even in his good works" (AE 40:295). Genuine penance consists of two parts. First is contrition and sorrow *coram deo* (before God). The second part of penance is faith that sins will be forgiven on account of Christ. Faith without contrition is presumption and carnal security.

From this vantage point, Melanchthon contrasts true Christian confession with papal confession. Evangelical confession is urged. Once again Melanchthon insists that "no one should be allowed to go to communion who has not been individually examined by his pastor to see if he is prepared to go to the holy sacrament" (AE 40:296). One is not to go the Sacrament as a matter of custom without knowing why he needs the Sacrament. The goal of the examination is repentance and faith in the words of the Absolution. In contrast to papal confession that adds satisfaction to contrition and faith, Melanchthon points to the atoning work of Christ, who has made satisfaction for our sins in our place.

The human order of the Church is a secondary matter governed by the apostle's words in 1 Corinthians 14:40 that "all things shall be done in order in the churches." Holy days are not abolished but are kept in Christian freedom so the Gospel might be proclaimed and taught. But they are not matters that should fragment the Church. Church order is differentiated from secular government. Masses and vigils for the dead should stop since the Sacrament of the Altar is not for the dead but the living.

Both Latin and German are permissible liturgical languages, but it is reasonable to use the vernacular so the common people understand and

---

7 For an overview of the practice of confession and absolution in the Reformation, see Ronald K Rittgers, *The Reformation of the Keys: Confession, Conscience and Authority in Sixteenth-Century Germany* (Cambridge: Harvard University Press, 2004).

are edified. Saints are honored when they are held up as a mirror of God's mercy and grace in Christ and when Christians exercise themselves in the faith and good works exemplified in the lives of the saints.

Marriage is to be honored as an estate instituted by God. Pastors are told to teach and act sympathetically in matters related to forbidden degrees of relationship in marriage. Christian liberty is to prevail, but not in a way that invites each to satisfy his own feelings. Each is to behave in a way that he may live with a clear conscience and serve the neighbor in love. The *Instructions* maintain that in cases where pastors are confused or uncertain in matters of casuistry, they should seek the counsel of those who are more learned or let the cases go to the appropriate authorities.[8]

The *Instructions* take up the question of the freedom of the will as Luther's work against Erasmus had occasioned debate within the Evangelical camp.[9] Melanchthon affirms the freedom of the will in external works—works regulated by law and punishment. In these things, which are "below" him, man has freedom. However the "righteousness of the flesh," which is a secular or civil righteousness, is not the righteousness that saves. When it comes to the righteousness of faith or saving righteousness before God, man is not free. He lacks the capacity to purify his heart. Without the Holy Spirit, the natural man cannot accomplish anything godly.

The section on Christian freedom is directed against antinomian mishandlings of the liberty granted by the Gospel. Positively, Melanchthon states that Christian freedom is the forgiveness of sins granted by the Spirit

8 Civil laws rightly govern marriage. This is reflected in Luther's *A Marriage Booklet for Simple Pastors* appended to the Small Catechism (see K-W, p. 367). Here Luther writes "'So many lands, so many customs,' says the common proverb. For this reason, because weddings and the married estate are worldly affairs, it behooves those of us who are 'spirituals' ("clergy") or ministers of the church in no way to order or direct anything regarding marriage, but instead to allow every city and land to continue their own customs that are now in use" (K-W, pp. 367–68). See the fine treatments by Scott Hendrix, "Luther on Marriage," *Lutheran Quarterly* (Autumn 2000): 335–50; James Nestingen, "Luther on Marriage, Vocation, and the Cross," *Word & World* (Winter 2003): 31–39; Oswald Bayer, "Luther's View of Marriage" in *Freedom in Response: Lutheran Ethics: Sources and Controversies* (Oxford: Oxford University Press, 2007), 169–82; and Carter Lindberg, "The Future of a Tradition: Luther and the Family" in *All Theology is Christology: Essays in Honor of David P. Scaer*, ed. Dean Wenthe et al. (Fort Wayne: Concordia Theological Seminary Press, 2000), 133–51. Lindberg writes, "Luther's application of evangelical theology to marriage and family desacramentalized marriage; desacralized the clergy and resacralized the life of the laity; opposed the maze of canonical impediments to marriage; strove to unravel the skein of canon law, imperial law, and German customs; and joyfully affirmed God's good creation, including sexual relations. In return, Luther was in such demand as a marriage counselor that he often complained of the burden imposed on him" (133).

9 See Luther's 1525 treatise on *The Bondage of the Will* (AE 33). Also see Robert Kolb, *Bound Choice, Election, and Wittenberg Theological Method: From Martin Luther to the Formula of Concord* (Grand Rapids: Eerdmans, 2005); Gerhard Forde, *The Captivation of the Will: Luther vs. Erasmus on Freedom and Bondage* (Grand Rapids: Eerdmans, 2005); and Hans Joachim Iwand, "The Freedom of the Christian and the Bondage of the Will," trans. Jacob Corzine, *Logia* (Eastertide 2008): 7–16.

without reference to human achievement. This freedom, he continues, means that Christ rules over the believer, protecting him against the power of the devil. The proclamation of this liberty should always carry with it a warning not to fall back into captivity to Satan and sin. Negatively, Christian liberty is not freedom from proper government and the payment of taxes. Melanchthon explains the application of Christian freedom in fasting and worship practices. The Christian is free from any obligation that would be imposed upon him with the promise of earning grace or meriting salvation.

A section on "The Turks" is an application of the teaching of the two governments. The government is given the power of the sword to defend, protect, and punish. Melanchthon dismisses as seditious any notion that Christians should not defend themselves against the Turk on the grounds that Christians should not take revenge on enemies. Just war may be waged. Christians are to pray for God's protection against this enemy even as they must be ready to defend their families against his assault.

"Daily Worship in the Church" provides general rubrics for Matins and Vespers. Instructions are given for preaching on Wednesdays and Fridays. Preachers are counseled in the selection of appropriate texts for the right proclamation of repentance and faith. Catechetical preaching on the Ten Commandments, Creed, and Lord's Prayer is urged for the sake of the children and unlearned. There should also be preaching on Baptism, the Sacrament of the Altar, and marriage. Festivals are to be celebrated without superstition. The Latin Introits, the Gloria Excelsis, Hallelujah, Sanctus, Agnus Dei, and simple sequences are recommended for high festivals. It is recognized that different forms of the Mass are in use and that this should not be a matter of agitation until greater uniformity can be achieved. Instructions are given for Christian burial[10] and practices surrounding childbirth.

Melanchthon then moves to a discussion of "The True Christian Ban." After a brief defense of right use of excommunication, Melanchthon rather abruptly takes up a treatment of the custom of ringing church bells, attempting to forestall unnecessary controversies and dispelling superstitious beliefs.

"The Office of Superintendent" is the pastor given responsibility in the region for the oversight of other clergy assuring that they preach God's

10 The Reformation transformed death and dying. See Austra Reinis, *Reforming the Art of Dying: The ars moriendi in the German Reformation (1519–1528)* (Burlington, Vermont: Ashgate Publishing Company, 2007); and Neil R. Leroux, *Martin Luther as Comforter: Writings on Death* (Leiden: Brill, 2007).

Word correctly and rightly administer the sacraments. Instructions are given for the discipline of preachers who err in doctrine or lead an ungodly and offensive life. The superintendent should examine candidates for ordination so churches are spared from incompetent pastors.[11]

A final section outlines the place of the school. After giving a rationale for education, namely, that young people are equipped for faithful service in church and state, Melanchthon goes on to provide a curriculum in three divisions embracing both spiritual and secular courses for study.

The Visitation

A general visitation of Saxony commenced in 1528 and continued with interruptions to 1531. The territory was divided into a number of circuits to be visited by teams composed of lay officials (jurists) and theologians. Armed with the *Instructions*, the visitors were to take stock of both spiritual and economic conditions in the region, working for unity in doctrine and practice between the churches. The practice of visitation would continue with a second round in 1533–1534. A third general visitation was taken in 1555. An attempt was made after the death of Elector August to advance Calvinistic theology in Saxony by the counselors who surrounded Christian the First, August's young son and successor. After Christian's death in 1591, his cousin, Duke Friedrich Wilhelm restored Lutheran theologians to their positions and commissioned the Wittenberg theologian Aegidius Hunnius (1550–1603) to compose articles of visitation to restore the theology of the Formula of Concord to the Saxon church.[12] This was done the next year in 1592. The practice would be incorporated in various territorial church orders and continue as a feature of Lutheran ecclesiastical life.

The Catechisms: A Fruit of the Visitation

Luther's own catechisms may be seen as a response to three events: (a) the request of Pastor Nicholas Hausmann for a catechism to use in the instruction of the "common folk" in 1524; (b) controversy between Agricola and Melanchthon on the place of the Law in the Christian life; and (c) a

11 "For the need of examination before a pastor is installed into office as well as the need of it in the further course of official activity is inextricably bound up with the specific duty to teach" (Elert, *The Structure of Lutheranism*, 351).

12 For the text of "The Saxon Visitation Articles of 1592" see Robert Kolb and James Nestingen, eds., *Sources and Context for the Book of Concord* (Minneapolis: Fortress Press, 2001), 256–61. These Articles were appended to the Book of Concord and were part of the visitation tradition that shaped the practice in the early Missouri Synod.

remedy to the maladies diagnosed in the visitations of 1528. The impact of the Saxon Visitations is seen in Luther's preface to the Small Catechism: "The deplorable, wretched deprivation that I recently encountered while I was a visitor has constrained and compelled me to prepare this catechism, or Christian instruction, in such a brief, plain, and simple version. Dear God, what misery I beheld! The ordinary person, especially in the villages, knows absolutely nothing about the Christian faith, and unfortunately many pastors are completely unskilled and incompetent teachers. Yet supposedly they all bear the name Christian, are baptized, and receive the holy sacrament, even though they do not know the Lord's Prayer, the Creed, or the Ten Commandments! As a result they live like simple cattle or irrational pigs and, despite the fact that the Gospel has returned, have mastered the fine art of misusing their freedom" (SC Preface; K-W, pp. 347–48).

Luther saw the catechism as a book to be used in home and congregation. "While Luther addressed the catechisms to pastors, he still envisioned the head of the household as the primary teacher."[13] James Nestingen observes that "The Small Catechism, in chart and pamphlet form, quickly became one of the most important documents of the Lutheran Reformation. It moved the village altar into the family kitchen, literally bringing instruction in the faith home to the intimacies of family life."[14] The careful literary craftsmanship evidenced in Luther's nuanced phrases and his repetition of key words made the catechism a useful tool for reinforcing the evangelical message that the laity heard from Saxon pulpits as God's Word echoed in ordinary households.

The catechism provided a basic summary of Christian doctrine along with a template for teaching. Luther outlines his pattern for catechesis in the Preface to the Small Catechism: (a) avoid changes or variations in the text; (b) after people have learned the text, teach them to understand it; and (c) once people have been taught the shorter catechism, take up the longer catechism (SC Preface; K-W, pp. 348–49). Luther intended the Small

---

13 Charles Arand, *That I May Be His Own: An Overview of Luther's Catechisms* (St. Louis: Concordia, 2000), 95.

14 James Nestingen, *Martin Luther: A Life* (Minneapolis: Fortress Press, 2003), 76.

Catechism to be a handbook for Christian doctrine, a prayer book, and a book for the ongoing Christian life.[15]

The theological structure of the Small Catechism is geared to the proper distinction of Law and Gospel. Luther departs from the traditional, medieval ordering of the chief parts as Lord's Prayer, Creed, and Ten Commandments. He explains his rationale for the sequencing of the Decalogue, Creed, and Our Father: "Thus the commandments teach man to recognize his sickness, enabling him to perceive what he must do or refrain from doing, consent to or refuse, and so he will recognize himself a sinful and wicked person. The Creed will teach and show him where to find the medicine—grace—which will help him to become devout and keep the commandments. The Creed points him to God and his mercy, given and made plain to him in Christ. Finally, the Lord's Prayer teaches all this, namely, through the fulfillment of God's commandments everything will be given him. In these three are the essentials of the entire Bible" (AE 43:14).

The core theological themes expressed in the visitation articles are expressed in the Small Catechism. The structure of the catechism itself follows the threefold shape of the Christian life: repentance, faith, and godly living. The Decalogue is preached to bring out about repentance. The Creed is the summary of the Trinitarian Gospel that creates faith. The Lord's Prayer is voice of faith. The sacraments strengthen faith. The daily prayers and table of duties are about the godly life, the vocation engendered by the Gospel as faith is active in love, calling upon the name of the Lord, and serving the neighbor in the stations of life. Even as the Saxon Visitation served to diagnose the maladies of parish life in early Lutheranism, so Luther's Catechisms, both Small and Large, served to address these deficiencies and guide both pastor and people to congregational, family, and personal life lived under the cross and in the hope of the resurrection.

15 The catechism looks at the concrete daily life of the simple Christian, taking both calling and estate into consideration, and understands them as the place in life God "gave us in the coordinate system of natural/creaturely, societal/social, as well as historical/cultural, relations." Albrecht Peters, *Commentary on Luther's Catechisms: Ten Commandments*, trans. Holger Sonntag (St. Louis: Concordia, 2009), 20. In this way the catechism teaches and exercises Christians in faith and love. "The catechism desires to instruct for this purpose, not only as a doctrinal, confessional book but also a book of prayer and comfort" (Peters, 20).

CHAPTER 2

Pastoral Care in Times of Anxiety and Distress

A Down-to-Earth Approach

Martin Luther was at his best at Christmas. With stark simplicity and yet profound insight, Luther's Christmas sermons speak of the lowliness of the Lord's birth in a way that prefigures the cross. The great German preacher of the twentieth century, Helmut Thielicke, was fond of saying that the "crib and the cross are of the same wood."[1] Luther also filtered his Christmas preaching through the cross where God's Son brought the incarnation to its real purpose: Christ's death for sinners. His ballad-like hymn "From Heaven Above to Earth I Come" tells the story of Christmas with striking beauty and clarity as it charts the trajectory of God drawing close to man, of God moving from heaven to earth:

> "Welcome to earth, O noble Guest,
> Through whom the sinful world is blest!
> You came to share my misery
> That You might share Your joy with me.
>
> Ah, Lord, though You created all,
> How weak You are, so poor and small,
> That You should choose to lay Your head
> Where lowly cattle lately fed!" (*LSB* 358:8–9)

Luther's memorable Christmas preaching and his poetic mastery of the story of Christ's birth would be put to use pastorally in his care for a young prince. Prince Joachim of Anhalt was twenty-six years old when Christmas came in 1535. For months he had battled with deep melancholy

1 Helmut Thielicke, *Being a Christian When the Chips are Down*, trans. H. George Anderson (Philadelphia: Fortress Press, 1979), 101.

and depression. Luther had spent time with the prince, praying for him and speaking the Lord's words of consolation and peace into his ears the previous summer. Yet Joachim's bouts with depression persisted. On December 25, 1535, Luther writes a tender but powerful letter to Joachim that resounds with the pure Gospel for those who are downcast and disillusioned in this season. "Our dear Lord Christ comfort Your Grace with his incarnation. He became incarnate to comfort and show his good will to all men, as the dear angels sing today, 'Glory to God in the highest, and on earth peace, good will toward men' " (Tappert, p. 98).

From heaven above, as Luther's hymn puts it, God comes to us. We need build no ladders to try vainly to climb into His heavenly presence. He comes not as an awesome deity with a majestic presence that terrifies but with mercy nestled down in a manger. This God is not our enemy but our Brother. He masks Himself with our humanity, dressing Himself in our flesh and blood. In this flesh and blood, He absorbs our sin and suffers and dies on the cross. Jesus is Immanuel, God with us, in our sin and shame. He is Immanuel in order that He might be God for us at Calvary. This Lord has not left the prince exiled in his holiday sadness. Luther puts the sermon of the first preachers of Christmas, the heavenly hosts who proclaimed the glad news of Jesus' birth to Bethlehem's shepherds, into Joachim's mind: God shows His favor to human beings in the sending of His Son. God, Luther reasons, would not bend down to us in such a friendly way if He was our enemy, if He was out to destroy us with His wrath.

How God is toward us we know from Jesus. Luther insisted that if you try to find God apart from Jesus, you end up only with the devil. Oswald Bayer observes that if we look for God within, we find only ghosts! Luther does not direct Joachim to his own thoughts or feelings. Instead he draws the prince away from self-absorbed reflection. Who God is and how He is disposed toward him, Joachim can know only from Mary's little baby. This knowledge of God cannot be found in nature or human rationality. There is no sentimental talk here of the presence of God in the cosmos everywhere available to seekers for the taking. It is not merely that God is present, for the presence of God without the cross and the word of promise would terrify and destroy us.

Luther cuts to the chase, reminding Joachim of what he has been taught: "If we are satisfied with the creed and the doctrine, what does it matter even if hell and all the devils fall upon us? What can distress us—other, perhaps, than our sins and bad conscience? Yet Christ has taken these from us, even while we sin daily. Who can terrify us except the devil? But greater than the devil is He that is in us, weak though our faith may be" (Tappert, p. 98). The baby of Bethlehem and the man of Calvary is God's Son. He came into the flesh to destroy the works of the devil. Our comfort is in the Creed's confession that God became man to suffer and die for sinners. Our confidence is in the doctrine, for this doctrine is not some humanly devised theory but the truth that God is for us in every way. Yes, the old evil foe may assault the conscience, stirring up the dregs of sins confessed and forgiven; he may haunt us with the phantoms of pained memory and ghosts of our own making. Mock and taunt us as he does with our weakness, Satan finally cannot harm us for we have another Lord. We have a Savior who nurses at Mary's breasts and hangs on a cross bruised and bloody. He holds on to us even when it appears that we can no longer find the strength to hold on to Him. Faith may be weak and wobbly, but Christ is strong and sure!

"We must be weak, and are willing to be," writes Luther, "in order that Christ's strength may dwell in us; as Saint Paul says, 'Christ's strength is made perfect in weakness' " (Tappert, p. 98). There are no shallow encouragements to muster up strength or to develop a more positive attitude. There are no calls in Luther's letter for Joachim to pull himself out of despondence and get in tune with the spirit of the season. Joachim is not counseled to get some help with his self-esteem issues. Luther comforts him instead with the words of the apostle. In weakness God puts His power to save on display. From the lowliness of the manger to the humiliation of the cross right down to the pit of Joachim's depression, God comes to save. God works in the depths. Luther once offended Erasmus by asserting that Christ Jesus is with us even in the sewer. Jesus is not ashamed to be found in the midst of barn flies and manure. He is not ashamed to be found in the company of weak sinners.

Consolation for Despair

Good pastor that he is, Luther does not try to lift Joachim's spirits with an appeal to the Law. "Don't you know that you should be rejoicing, after all it is Christmas, dear Prince." There is none of that in Luther's letter. Instead, there is the comfort of Christmas. It is the consolation of a Christ who makes Himself to be a friend of sinners, joining Himself to them in their weakness and misery.

Luther fortifies Joachim to rest in the promises of this Christ, to let himself be weak so that Christ can be his strength: "Your Grace has not yet betrayed or crucified the dear Lord. Even if Your Grace had, Christ nevertheless remains gracious. He prayed even for those who crucified him. Therefore, be of good cheer. In the strength of Christ resist the evil spirit, who can do no more than trouble, terrify, or slay" (Tappert, p. 98). Joachim should not rely on his own reason or strength but on the strength of Christ Jesus who has called him by the Gospel to live in His kingdom in everlasting righteousness, innocence, and blessedness. Only in this Lord can demonic darkness of doubt be dispelled. Luther presses the promises of Christ into the depths of Joachim's melancholy that, even in these dark and shadowy regions, he might know the peace of Christ and hold fast to Him.

Another example of Luther's pastoral care for a person suffering from chronic bouts with melancholy and spiritual depression can be seen in his work with Jerome Weller (1499–1572). Weller was a young man who came to Wittenberg to study law but altered his academic path to study theology, spending eight years at the university.[2] He lived for a time in Luther's home while tutoring Luther's children. He was often plagued by depression and temptations to despair and unbelief. Luther learned of Jerome's condition while he was away at Coburg in the summer of 1530 awaiting the outcome of the Diet of Augsburg. In July, Luther writes Weller a letter that is both consoling and rich in practical advice.

After reminding Weller that temptation itself is not a sign of unbelief but of faith, Luther urges him to rejoice in this trial, for it indicates that he belongs to Christ. Satan has no need of enticing or ensnaring those who already belong to him. Temptation's target is always the First Commandment as the devil seeks to divorce the believer from Christ Jesus and lure him into the kingdom of darkness. In fact, Luther says that such temptation is a necessity for the Christian, more so "than food and drink" (Tappert, p. 85).

Luther advises Weller to know the tactics that Satan uses in temptation. He is told to recognize the tempter for what he is, the roaring lion described in 1 Peter 5:8. Drawing on his own seasoned experience as a warrior against the old evil foe, Luther recognizes the strategic maneuvers of the enemy: "I know the wiles of the devil. If he cannot break a person with his first attack, he tries by persevering to wear him out and weaken him until the person falls and confesses himself beaten" (Tappert, p. 85). The persistence of Satan must be countered by the persistence of faith that clings to the promises of the Gospel and not by a reliance on one's own resources.

With a sharp eye toward the reality of the devil's works and ways, Luther provides some tips for Jerome. He counsels Jerome to "avoid entering a disputation with the devil and do not allow yourself to dwell

2 For more on Weller, see Martin Brecht, *Martin Luther: Shaping and Defining the Reformation 1521–1532* (Minneapolis: Fortress Press, 1993), 378–79.

on those deadly thoughts, for to do so is nothing short of yielding to the devil and letting him have his way" (Tappert, p. 85). Rather than arguing with the devil, Luther advises Jerome to show his enemy contempt and scorn. The devil is no friend of humor when it is at his expense: "In this sort of temptation and struggle, contempt is the best and easiest method of winning over the devil. Laugh your adversary to scorn and ask him who it is with whom you are talking. By all means flee solitude, for the devil watches and lies in wait for you most of all when you are alone. The devil is conquered by mocking and despising him, not by resisting and arguing with him. Therefore, Jerome, joke and play games with my wife and others. In this way you will drive out your diabolical thoughts and take courage" (Tappert, p. 85).

Luther recognizes that the retreat into solitude can be especially problematic for it is in this loneliness that dreaded anxieties are likely to be magnified and darkened. So Luther counsels Jerome: "Whenever the devil pesters you with these thoughts, at once seek out the company of men, drink more, joke and jest, or engage in some other form of merriment. Sometimes it is necessary to drink a little more, play, jest, or even commit some sin in defiance and contempt of the devil in order not to give him an opportunity to make us scrupulous about trifles. We shall be overcome if we worry too much about falling into some sin" (Tappert, p. 86). No one can ever accuse Luther or being puritanical or pietistic. Since the Christian is freed in Christ by the forgiveness of sins, Luther sees that a timid Christian like Jerome is easily intimidated by the devil and drawn into captivity. Luther knows that if Jerome cloisters himself in loneliness and in the austerity of his own efforts to win victory over demonic accusations, he will be easily overcome by the cunning of Satan. His own efforts at abiding by the Law of God are fragmentary and incomplete, hardly capable of withstanding the devil's sharp eye for an undefended point of entry.

Here Luther moves to tutor Jerome in the essential distinction for survival on the spiritual battlefield, the ability to discern the difference between the Law and the Gospel. Luther is consummately bold in exercising Jerome in this distinction. So he tells Jerome, "If the devil should say, 'Do not drink,' you should reply to him, 'On this very account, because you forbid it, I shall drink, and what is more, I shall drink a generous amount.' Thus one must always do the opposite of what Satan prohibits" (Tappert, p. 86). Luther's playfulness in this letter should not be taken as an example of the reformer's tumble into the gutter of antinomian excessiveness. Instead, he is tutoring Jerome in how to use the Law and the Gospel against the tempter, who ultimately despises them both.

When Satan comes to attack, the Law is of no benefit. The tempted person knows well what the Law commands and forbids, but knowledge of the Law does not equal the ability to keep its divine requirements. Luther recognizes that the devil is a skilled and clever attorney, capable of producing embarrassing and condemning evidence to convict the sinner. Hence Luther admonishes Jerome never to argue with the devil: "When the devil attacks and torments us, we must completely set aside the whole Decalogue. When the devil throws our sins up to us and declares that we deserve death and hell, we ought to speak thus: 'I admit that I deserve death and hell. What of it? Does this mean that I shall be sentenced to eternal damnation? By no means. For I know One who suffered and made satisfaction in my behalf. His name is Jesus Christ, the Son of God. Where he is, there I shall be also" (Tappert, pp. 86–87).[3] In this way Luther urges Jerome not to put his confidence in his own paltry efforts at obedience to God's Law but to anchor his trust in the obedience of Christ who is our righteousness.

A troubled conscience does not need moral instruction or lessons in Christian ethics but the forgiveness of sins. Luther knows the deceptiveness of the conscience, as it can be tender and sensitive to the sin that is ever present or it can be hardened in the attempt to excuse sin rather than repent. So Luther urges Christ alone into the conscience of Jerome.

Jerome's case was not an isolated episode for Luther. There is a Table Talk from December 1531 where Luther deals with a similar theme as he engages in a conversation with John Schlaginhaufen, who, like Jerome, also lived for a time in Luther's household and suffered from depression. Schlaginhaufen recounts that Luther cites 2 Corinthians 12:9 in assuring him that God's strength is made manifest in human weakness. It is in the frailty of our humanity when there are no fleshly resources to draw upon that God demonstrates His power to redeem and rescue.

In this Table Talk, Luther strings together a number of biblical texts from both and Old and New Testaments to instruct and encourage

---

3 Luther's advice to Jerome found its way into the *Lutheran Service Book: Pastoral Care Companion* (St. Louis: Concordia, 2007). Note the counsel given to pastors in the section on "Guilt and Shame": "The conscience terrified by the memories of sin finds itself living under the condemnation of the Law, which offers no peace or rest. For the Christian who is driven by the Law to despair of the mercies of Christ Jesus, the pastor must 'set the whole Decalogue aside' (Luther) and make the most of the Gospel. The pastor will guide the besieged Christian to find consolation in the word of absolution, a word that provides forgiveness for the guilty and covering for those who stand in shame on account of their sin" (307). This is not "antinomianism" but a profoundly evangelically pastoral necessity. Also see Bryan Wolfmueller, "The Highest Art in Christendom: Recovering the Difficulty of Distinguishing Law and Gospel" in *Theology Is Eminently Practical: Essays in Honor of John T. Pless*, eds. Jacob Corzine and Bryan Wolfmueller (Fort Wayne: Lutheran Legacy Press, 2012), 257–71.

Schlaginhaufen. Luther uses these passages to impress on his table companion the truth of Romans 15:4, that these inspired writings were written to give us hope: " 'Whatever things were written aforetime were written for us that we through patience,' etc. Abraham, Isaac, Jacob, the dear Joseph, Rebecca, and Leah have no idea whatsoever that we are today reading narratives about them. David does not know that we have his psalms in Germany and that we find comfort in them even as he did long ago. The Lord helped David, who put his trust in God. So he will also aid us who hope in him, for his word is yea and amen" (Tappert, pp. 87–88). The Holy Scriptures for Luther are not a "mausoleum of the Spirit" (Schleiermacher) but rather the "breathing place" of the Spirit, the location of the Spirit's present work in and through the inspired words of the Bible.[4] Luther makes a lively use of the Holy Scripture precisely because its words are spirit and truth, living and pulsating with the very Spirit who is the Lord and Giver of Life. Luther brings the words of scriptural promise into the present tense, directing them into the concrete situation of his hearer so that he might be built up and enabled to stand against the attacks of the evil one in the midst of tribulation. The Holy Scriptures interpret our suffering in light of God's steadfast mercy and compassion revealed in them.

God's Love/Hate Relationship with Afflictions

"God both loves and hates our afflictions. He loves them when they provoke us to prayer. He hates them when we are driven to despair by them" (Tappert, p. 87). Luther then cites specific biblical references to drive home this point. Coupling Psalm 50:23 ("The one who offers thanksgiving as his sacrifice glorifies Me") with Psalm 51:17 ("The sacrifices of God are a broken spirit and a contrite heart"), Luther seeks to demonstrate that, even in the brokenness of affliction, the believer renders his life to God in the confidence that the Lord will remain true to His word and not cast off those who hope in His mercy. Luther does not attempt to trivialize the pain nor does he offer stoic-sounding advice to endure detached from the reality of one's situation. Instead the broken heart is offered up to God knowing that "the Lord hears the gentle sighs of the afflicted" (Tappert, p. 87).

One of the aspects of Luther's pastoral care is his rhetorical ability to paint word pictures and use images. Luther's skillful use of this aspect can be seen in this Table Talk as he urges Schlaginhaufen to "excommunicate" the demonic temptations that assault his soul, for they are counterfeit

4 Here see the Oswald Bayer, "Luther as Interpreter of Holy Scripture," in *The Cambridge Companion to Martin Luther*, ed. Donald K. McKim (Cambridge: Cambridge University Press, 2003), 73–85.

currency: "If these temptations do not let up, excommunicate them in the name of the Lord Jesus Christ and say: 'God has forbidden us to accept these coins of yours. They do not come from Hungary or Bohemia or Saxony but were struck by the devil.' Therefore, we are to refuse his coins and not accept them from him" (Tappert, p. 88). In this way, Luther engages in pastoral conversation using simple but striking images of excommunication and worthless coins to prepare his friend to face the spiritual struggles which had overtaken him.

On October 7, 1534, Luther wrote a letter to Matthias Weller (1507–1563) who like his older brother, Jerome, also suffered from bouts with depression. The younger Weller was a talented musician and served for a time as the organist in the cathedral church in Freiberg. Recognizing this connection to music, Luther counsels Weller to follow the example of the Old Testament saints, rejoicing in the Lord by means of song: "When you are sad, therefore, and when melancholy threatens to get the upper hand, say: 'Arise! I must play a song unto the Lord on my regal [a portable organ] (be it the *Te Deum laudamus* or the *Benedictus*), for the Scriptures teach us that it pleases him to hear a joyful song and the music of stringed instruments.' Then begin striking the keys and singing in accompaniment, as David and Elisha did, until your sad thoughts vanish. If the devil returns and plants worries and sad thoughts in your mind, resist him manfully and say, 'Begone, devil! I must now play and sing unto my Lord Christ' " (Tappert, p. 97).

As with Jerome, Luther urges Matthias to seek out the company of others. Here as with other instances of people suffering from depression, Luther pays attention to their social circumstances. Werner Elert observes that "Luther remained convinced that man's sadness is 'natural'; that is, connected with sin's corruption of nature. Luther saw sadness as a downright 'tool' of the devil. . . . He knows that sadness thrives best in solitude."[5] So Luther directs Matthias to listen to the voices of his fellow Christians and forsake his own morbid thoughts.

Left in solitude, the mind is unguarded against the devil who would plant seeds of destructive despondence, which darkens thinking. Rather than sitting in loneliness and pondering these demonically induced thoughts, Matthias is told to seek out the companionship of others who can cheer him with their testimony to God's comfort. This is more than mundane psychological advice; Luther sees it as an active way to defy Satan: "In such fashion you must learn to oppose him and not permit him

5 Werner Elert, *The Structure of Lutheranism*, trans. Walter Hansen (St. Louis: Concordia, 1962), 467.

to put thoughts in your mind. If you allow one thought to enter, and you pay attention to it, he will force ten additional thoughts into your mind until at last he overpowers you. Therefore the best thing you can do is to rap the devil on the nose at the very start. Act like that man who, whenever his wife began to nag and snap at him, drew out his flute from under his belt and played merrily until she was exhausted and let him alone. So you must turn to your regal or gather some good companions about you and sing with them until you know how to defy the devil" (Tappert, p. 97).

Luther is encouraging Matthias to make use of the "mutual consolation of the brethren" as he is to receive God's words of comfort from their lips. Even if Matthias is unable to stand on his own two feet, so to speak, he can lean on Christian friends: "If you are convinced that such thoughts come from the devil, you have already gained the victory. But since you are still weak in your faith, listen to us, who by God's grace know it, and lean on our staff until you learn to walk by yourself. And when good people comfort you, my dear Matthias, learn to believe that God is speaking to you through them. Pay heed to them and have no doubt that it is most certainly God's word, coming to you according to God's command through men, that comforts you" (Tappert, p. 97).

Although Luther does not make a direct citation of the apostle Paul's words in 2 Corinthians 1:4 that we are to comfort others in their afflictions even as we have been comforted by God, this Pauline thought certainly informs Luther's approach. God's Word comes in human speech so Matthias is instructed to receive the evangelical words spoken by his friends as the Lord's own words. Matthias is to trust in them and not in the deceptive impulses to unbelief that war against faith. Recognizing these temptations as wrought by Satan, Matthias should counter them with a reliance on Christ's promises spoken and sung in the company of other Christians.

Philip Melanchthon, Luther's colleague, was prone to bouts of anxiety and worry. Hidden away at the Castle Coburg in the summer of 1530 while the Diet of Augsburg was in progress, Luther provides pastoral counsel for his co-worker in a series of letters. Just two days after the evangelical party had presented the Augsburg Confession to Emperor Charles, Luther writes Melanchthon seeking to alleviate his worries, reminding him that Christ Jesus is the Lord of His Church. The "Lutheran" cause is in His hands.

Luther rebukes Melanchthon for his unbelief. He states that Melanchthon's worries have gained the upper hand: "They rule your heart, not on account of the greatness of the cause but by reason of the greatness of your unbelief" (Tappert, p. 146). After he reminds his colleague of God's promises in Scripture (Psalm 55:22; 145:18), Luther says "Why, then, are you constantly tormenting yourself? If our cause is false, let us recant. But if it is true, why should we make Him a liar who has given us such great promises and who commands us to be confident and undismayed?" (Tappert, p. 146). Satan is supplied with too many weapons by Melanchthon's faithless fears. "I pray for you very earnestly, and I am deeply pained that you keep sucking up cares like a leech and thus rendering my prayers vain. Christ knows whether it comes from stupidity or the Spirit, but I for my part am not very much troubled about our cause" (Tappert, p. 147). Luther reminds Melanchthon that Satan can do no more than kill the body. God is able to raise the dead. He is the source of our confidence even if the confessional cause fails.

Complaining that writing Melanchthon is "like pouring water into the sea" (Tappert, p. 147), Luther threatens to come to Augsburg himself if he hears that Melanchthon is not doing well. This would give him opportunity to see "Satan's formidable teeth round about" (Tappert, p. 147).

After receiving a copy of the Augsburg Confession, Luther writes another letter to Melanchthon on June 29, 1530. In this letter, Luther approves the confession and notes nothing more could be conceded to the papists. Luther notes that he has endured torment in body and spirit. Luther recognizes the vexing power of the evil one and makes light of the foe: "I am well aware that he has sworn to kill me and will not rest until he devours me. But if he does so, he will swallow a purgative, God willing, that will burst his belly" (Tappert, p. 149).[6] The message of Acts 14:22—that the kingdom is entered only through much tribulation—is a reality. Faith comprehends all things including that which is unseen. Luther recalls God's deliverance of Moses from Pharaoh as an example.

A letter of July 31, 1530, to Melanchthon, continues to encourage steadfastness. "I believe that you have wrestled manfully with the demons this past week. . . . I am with you in faith and spirit as much as I am able. But I believe that the frail Christ is with you even more" (Tappert, p. 154). Luther continues to pray that Melanchthon would remain steadfast and not cover up the pope's abominations. Once again Luther refers to the messenger of Satan who buffets his flesh in a reference to 2 Corinthians 12:7. Referencing John 10:29, Psalm 126:1, and Psalm 55:22, Luther commits Melanchthon and their cause to God. Luther concludes the letter

6 Luther's language is colorful to the point of being humorous as he describes himself as a bowel-busting laxative. Luther often uses humor as a tool for pastoral care. For more on this point, see "Facetious Pastoral Care" in Eric Gritsch, *The Wit and Wisdom of Martin Luther* (Minneapolis: Fortress Press, 2006), 57–64.

expressing his confidence in the sufficiency of Christ's victory: "[I write] from the castle that is full of demons but where Christ reigns in the midst of his enemies" (Tappert, p. 155).

Luther writes Conrad Cordatus (c. 1480–1546) on December 3, 1544.[7] Cordatus, a pastor in Brandenburg, is at the point of despair. In the midst of persecution, God calls us to rejoice. Luther cites Luke 21:17 and Matthew 5:12 to console Cordatus. The prince of this world is a "mere vapor" (Tappert, p. 169) compared with Christ. Christ will triumph. Christians rule in the midst of their enemies: "Outwardly we are living in the kingdom of the devil, and so we should not expect to see and hear good things on the outside. But inwardly we are living in the Kingdom of Christ, where we may behold the riches of God's glory and grace" (Tappert, p. 170). The hatred that Christians experience from the unbelieving world is not unexpected, for it is actually directed at the "master of the house," Christ: "It is our glory, and yours, that we let the unclouded sun of our doctrine rise on the godless and ungrateful world in accordance with the example of our Father, who makes this his sun to rise on the evil and on the good. And since the sun of our doctrine is his, there is no wonder that those of the household who hate the master of the house also hate our doctrine" (Tappert, p. 170). Luther uses allusions to 2 Corinthians 6:8 to cheer Cordatus. "But we shall make our way through glory and shame, through good report and evil report, through hate and love, through friends and foes, until we arrive where there are none but friends, in the Kingdom of the Father" (Tappert, p. 170).

It is the devil who stands behind anxiety and worry with his convincing propaganda aimed at subverting the trustworthiness of the divine promise. Luther would have the Christian live in the awareness of the devil's lying tactics and be prepared to confront him with the strong weaponry of the Gospel. This means that the Christian is to be guided by the proper distinction of the Law from the Gospel so that his final appeal is not to his works or piety but to Christ alone. This is a struggle that is persistent in this life; it will not be finished until the Christian is brought through death to the perfection of the resurrection. It is not a battle that the believer engages in isolation. Surrounded by the company of Christ's holy people and sharing with them a single Baptism and faith, the believer is enabled to stand in defiance of the evil one.[8]

---

7 For more on Cordatus's life, see Robert Rosin, "Conrad Cordatus" in *The Oxford Encyclopedia of the Reformation*, vol. 1, ed. Hans J. Hillerbrand (Oxford: Oxford University Press, 1996), 430.

8 Here also see John A. Maxfield, "Genesis as the History of the Church Between God and the Devil," in *Luther's Lectures on Genesis and the Formation of Evangelical Identity* (Kirksville, MO: Truman State University Press, 2008), 147–151.

CHAPTER 3

Pastoral Care in the Face of Doubt and Despair

Christ Alone

An example of Luther's pre-Reformation pastoral care is found in a letter to George Spenlein, written in 1516 (Tappert, p. 109). Spenlein was a friar in the Augustinian monastery in Wittenberg. Of this letter, Brecht writes, "It also shows that Luther had become critical of the meritorious righteousness that one was supposed to create for one's self, and therefore he desired to rely on the gift of God's righteousness, though this was not very easy for him."[1] In this letter, Luther urges his friend to learn to despair of self and trust only in Christ crucified.

The recognition of one's state as a sinner does not lead to despair but opens the way to recognize Christ as the companion of sinners. Luther counsels his monastic colleague to "beware of aspiring to such purity that you will not wish to be looked upon as a sinner, or to be one. For Christ only dwells in sinners. On this account he descended from heaven, where he dwelt among the righteous, to dwell among sinners. Meditate on this love of his and you will see his sweet consolation. For why was it necessary for him to die if we can obtain a good conscience by our works and afflictions? Accordingly you will find peace only in him and only when you despair of yourself and your own works. Besides you will learn from him that just as he received you, so he has made your sins his own and has made his righteousness yours" (Tappert, p. 110).

When we are deprived of self-righteousness, the righteousness of Christ enables us to bear with the weak and help them: "Cursed is the righteousness of the man who is unwilling to assist others on the ground that they are worse than he is and who thinks of fleeing from and forsaking those whom he ought now be helping with patience, prayer, and example" (Tappert, p. 111). Christian life is not lived in a sterile environment that

1 Brecht, *Martin Luther: His Road to Reformation* (Minneapolis: Fortress Press, 1993), 156.

spares the believer contact with flesh and blood sinners. Luther gently reminds Spenlein, "If you are a lily and a rose of Christ, therefore, know that you will live among thorns" (Tappert, p. 111). At this early "pre-Reformation" stage in his career, Luther shows signs of the direction in which his theology is moving as it focuses on the necessity of Christ's atoning death and the sufficiency of the Lord's righteousness for sinners who have no righteousness of their own. The way of faith is not confidence in the self but trust in the merit of Christ alone. These early, brotherly admonitions to a fellow friar will come to full fruition in the reformer's maturing pastoral work.

Predestination: Terror or Comfort?

An issue that seems to repeat itself for Luther is anxiety and doubt related to the biblical teaching of divine election or predestination. A laywoman, Barbara Lisskirchen, was troubled over the doctrine of predestination, a doctrine that has broken many hearts and heads by inviting anxious speculation. In a letter to Barbara, Luther counsels her to consider this doctrine evangelically. Elert comments on Luther's doctrine of predestination: "Peace of conscience, which is the important matter here, is not the false security of synergism—just as it should not be the false security of a fatalistic belief in salvation."[2]

Luther lifts up four items for Barbara's consideration. First, he identifies her temptation as a hellish invitation to unbelief from the devil himself. It is a "fiery dart" from the evil one (Ephesians 6:16) that Luther had himself experienced. It is a temptation to investigate the secret things of God. Luther uses Psalm 131:1 (my eyes are not raised too high; I do not occupy myself with things too great for me) to direct Barbara away from what God has concealed from human eyes and is inaccessible to human reason. We are not to pry into the majesty of God. Second, Barbara is to learn to ask herself "in which commandment is it written that I should think about and deal with this matter?" She is to use the First Commandment against Satan in this act of spiritual warfare. Third, if the tormenting thoughts continue, she is to be persistent and refuse to give up. "In this way you must always put these thoughts away from you and turn your attention to God's Commandments" (Tappert, p. 116). Fourth, she is to focus on Christ crucified. "The highest of all God's commands is this, that we hold before

---

2 Werner Elert, *The Structure of Lutheranism*, trans. Walter Hansen (St. Louis: Concordia, 1962), 130. Also see Fredrik Brosché, *Luther on Predestination* (Stockholm: Almqvist and Wiksell, International, 1978).

our eyes the image of his dear Son, our Lord Jesus Christ" (Tappert, p. 117). This fourth point, Luther weaves into the concluding benediction: "May our dear Lord Jesus Christ show you his hands and his side and gladden your heart with his love, and may you behold and hear him until you find your joy in him" (Tappert, p. 117). He ends with an allusion to John 20:27.

A Table Talk recorded by Conrad Cordatus in the autumn of 1532 also takes up predestination. Luther cautions that the Christian ought to avoid disputing with himself about predestination for "it is like a fire that cannot be extinguished." Instead, the believer is directed to the Means of Grace: "Our Lord God is so hostile to such disputation that he instituted Baptism, the Word, and the Sacraments as signs to counteract it" (Tappert, p. 122).

In this discourse, Luther urges his hearers to approach the teaching of election in and through Christ. We do not use the doctrine of election as a teaching that is preliminary to Christ, but instead we understand it as a corollary of the fact that Christ alone is the Lord who saves sinners. Using the New Testament's imagery of Christ alone as the foundation, Luther remarks that Christians start with the foundation (Christ) and not the roof (predestination): "In Christ, God has furnished us with a foundation, on which to stand and from which we can go up to heaven. He is the only way and the only gate which leads to the Father. If we despise this foundation and in the devil's name start building at the roof, we shall surely fall" (Tappert, p. 122).

In caring for Christians plagued by doubt or despair, Luther directs the perplexed and doubting away from self to the righteousness of Jesus Christ for sinners. In his 1535 commentary on Galatians, Luther writes: "This is why our theology is certain: it snatches us away from ourselves and places us outside ourselves, so that we do not depend on our own strength, conscience, experience, person, or works but depend on that which is outside ourselves, that is, on the promise and truth of God, which cannot deceive" (AE 27:387). Using the language of the cross and the wounds of Christ, Luther directs those who are tormented by doubts or tempted to despair of God's mercy to the atonement. It is only in Jesus' death for sinners that we have forgiveness of sins and, with that forgiveness, the peace of God that transcends both rationality and experience. The paradox of *deus crucifixus* (God crucified) finds the glory of God in the suffering of Christ. "Therefore in Luther's sense the question that has arisen—what assurance the Christian has that his belief in the forgiveness of sins does not rest on an illusion—must be answered very generally by pointing to

Christ. He is the basis of the knowledge of the faith in God's readiness to forgive sins."[3]

Another Table Talk recorded by Veit Dietrich in August 1533 again deals with the doctrine of election. Here Luther counsels those who are troubled about the certainty of their salvation because they do not experience peace. Luther reminds his audience that the Christian life is lived amidst trials, afflictions, and crosses. The peace of Romans 5:1 is not to be confused with any form of worldly tranquility, even "peace of mind." The Christian will not be without temptation in this life, even the temptation to despair of God's mercy, of being driven by unsettled and chaotic emotions. Luther alludes to Matthew 11:5 when he notes that Christians are precisely the "poor" who have the good news preached to them when he says, "Because Christians always feel sorrows and afflictions, therefore, it is the prime precept of God that we encourage and console the afflicted who are in sorrow. And on the other hand, those who are thus tempted should allow themselves to be cheered and should put an end to their depression and fear" (Tappert, p. 124).

The Table Talk recorded by Caspar Heydenreich on February 18, 1542, sets forth Luther's response to those who use the doctrine of election for speculation rather than faith. Luther warns against an "epicurean" approach that is nothing more than fatalism. Such a fatalistic approach casts aside the Passion of Christ and the Sacraments. It is the work of the devil to make us unbelieving and doubtful. It would be foolish of God to give us His Son and the Scriptures if He wished us to be uncertain or doubtful of salvation.

God is truthful, and His truth gives us certainty. A distinction must be made, Luther asserts, between the knowledge of God and the despair of God. We know nothing of the unrevealed God, the hidden God. God blocks the path here. "We must confess that what is beyond our comprehension is nothing for us to bother about" (Tappert, p. 132). We are to stick with the revealed God. "He who inquires into the majesty of God shall be crushed by it" (Tappert, p. 132). God gives us His Son so that we may know that we are saved. Hence we are "to begin at the bottom with the incarnate Son and with your terrible original sin" (Tappert, p. 133). We are to stick with Baptism and the preaching of God's Word.

The doctrine of election is not to be used for speculation. Only in the Word and Baptism does the believer find comfort when facing the troubling thoughts that come from Satan himself. This satanic temptation is aimed at the First Commandment. This temptation is a reenactment of Genesis 3.

3 Elert, *The Structure of Lutheranism,* 108.

Werner Elert observes: "The thought of predestination can by no means provide a foundation for faith, but that faith must already be in existence if the thought of predestination is to be at all bearable."[4]

When he turns to his own experience, Luther recalls the consolation he received from Staupitz when vexed by the question of election. Staupitz directed him to the wounds of Christ wherein we have the mercy of God revealed; God is surely there for us. The example of Adam and Eve is a warning against every attempt to find God apart from His Word, for such an endeavor is more than spiritually frustrated; it ends in unbelief. Instead, God wraps Himself in His promises of mercy and grace, and He will not let sinners access Him in a place other than His Gospel: "Without the Word there is neither faith nor understanding. This is the invisible God. The path is blocked here. Such was the answer which the apostles received when they asked Christ when he would restore the kingdom to Israel, for Christ said, 'It is not for you to know.' Here God desires to be inscrutable and to remain incomprehensible" (Tappert, p. 132). Apart from the baby of Bethlehem, who goes on to suffer and die as the man of Calvary, God remains an evasive presence whose ways are inexplicable and whose power is condemnation.

No comfort is to be found in the "hidden God" (*deus absonditus*) but only in the "revealed God" (*deus revelatus*) that is in Christ. Hence theology and pastoral care begin below at the manger and the cross and not above in the majesty that terrifies. "Paul . . . desires to teach Christian theology, which does not begin above in the utmost heights, like all other religions, but below in the profoundest depths. . . . If you are concerned with your salvation, forget about all ideas of law, all philosophical doctrines, and hasten to the crib and to his mother's bosom and see him, an infant, a growing child, a dying man. Then you will be able to escape all fear and errors. This vision will keep you on the right way. He [Luther] says the same in the briefest possible formula: 'To seek God outside of Jesus is the Devil.' "[5]

A Table Talk recorded by Conrad Cordatus in the autumn of 1531 addresses those who are tempted by doubt and despair. Luther advises that people beset with such temptations should avoid solitude and seek

4 Elert, *The Structure of Lutheranism,* 122. Luther's 1525 book against Erasmus, *On the Bondage of the Will*, is foundational for Luther's pastoral approach to this issue. Here "Erasmus set out to win a debate. Luther sought to comfort and rescue the lost." Gerhard Forde, *The Captivation of the Will* (Grand Rapids: Eerdmans, 2005), 25.

5 Gerhard Ebeling, *Luther: An Introduction to His Thought,* trans. R. A. Wilson (Philadelphia: Fortress, 1972), 235.

out conversation with others about the Psalms and the Scriptures. Luther reminds his table companions that human powers are not sufficient to overcome doubt. Do not dwell on these thoughts. Trust in God's Word knowing that Satan will try to wear down by relentless perseverance those he cannot take by force or cunning. He directs his hearers away from their own thoughts to the Scriptures, recognizing that "dwelling on these thoughts, wrestling with them, wishing to conquer them or wishing idly for them to come to an end will only make them more disturbing and strengthen them unto perdition without providing a remedy" (Tappert, p. 118). In this Table Talk, Luther recollects how Pastor Bugenhagen comforted him, reminding him: "You ought not to despise my consolation because I am convinced that I speak words of God from heaven" (Tappert, p. 118). Luther exhorts his companions to rely on God's Word in these seasons of temptation when Satan is persistent in his devilish tactics to wear beleaguered believers down if he "cannot take suddenly by force or cunning" (Tappert, p. 119).

Luther warns Valentine Hausmann, a burgomaster in Freiberg, not to be overly concerned by his doubts and bouts with unbelief. God deals with us in wondrous ways. These afflictions are like Paul's thorn in the flesh, for they drive us to cry out to the Lord for mercy. Worry over unbelief is a sign that God has not forsaken you, Luther tells Hausmann. In this striking letter, Luther counsels Hausmann to "accept this scourge as laid upon you by God for your own good, even as Saint Paul had to bear a thorn in the flesh, and thank God that he deems you worthy of such unbelief and terror, for they will drive you more to pray and seek help" (Tappert, p. 119). Luther writes that Hausmann is to learn to cry out with the disciples, "Lord, help thou my unbelief" (Mark 9:24). Hausmann is instructed not to become impatient because his faith seems weak. Rather, he is to call upon the Father in prayer and cling to His Word.

Hausmann is experiencing what Luther identifies as *Anfechtung.* The word *Anfechtung* has no exact English equivalent. It encompasses doubts, spiritual turmoil, desolation, despair, and desperation. Alister McGrath notes that for Luther *Anfechtung* is constituted in two distinct but inseparable aspects: "objective" assaults of spiritual forces on the believer from outside and the "subjective" stress and anxiety these assaults create internally.[6] Dennis Ngien observes that Luther regarded *Anfechtung*

---

6 Alister McGrath, *Luther's Theology of the Cross* (Oxford: Basil Blackwell, 1985), 170.

as "delicious despair," for hidden within is "God's delightful comfort."[7] Luther says in the Genesis lectures: "When God works, He turns His face away at first and seems to be the devil, not God" (AE 7:103).

Five months later, Luther writes a second letter to Valentine Hausmann. In this letter he continues to encourage him to remember the long-suffering mercy of God: "God is not the kind of father who casts off sick and erring children; if he were, he would have no children" (Tappert, p. 121). Luther tells Hausmann to cry out against this "terror" using the Lord's Prayer in resistance of the devil. If his spiritual condition is such that he cannot pray for himself, Luther encourages him simply to listen to the voice of another read the Psalms or New Testament texts for him. Here we may observe that Luther sees spiritual struggles as ongoing and not remedied by simplistic solutions. In the face of chronic bouts with the devil's attack on the conscience, the embattled believer is tutored to use the weaponry of God's promises and prayer.

The Evangelical Use of Prayer

A further fruit of the Small Catechism in the life of prayer can be seen in Luther's celebrated letter to his friend, the Wittenberg barber, Peter Beskendorf. Given the title *A Simple Way to Pray*, this tract of 1535 demonstrates how Luther uses the Catechism to teach Christians how to pray. "Nowhere is the connection between order and freedom in Luther's practice so clearly seen as in his advice for Master Peter" says Martin Brecht.[8]

The letter to Peter the Barber is an "open letter" giving evangelical instruction on prayer. Here we see Luther as the pastoral catechist. Luther provides pastoral advice on the practice of prayer. A set discipline and routine is helpful. "It is a good thing to let prayer be the first business of the morning and the last at night" (AE 43:193). Prayer, however, is not limited to particular times and places. For the believer, "work is prayer," but for the unbeliever "work is nothing but cursing." Christians "pray

7 Dennis Ngien, *Luther as Spiritual Advisor: The Interface of Theology and Piety in Luther's Writings* (London: Paternoster Press, 2007), 131. Also note the observation of Klaus Schwarzwäller: "[Luther] experienced it as torture, yet for him this *Anfechtung* stands along with prayer and meditation as indispensable in dealing with Holy Scriptures. In his translation of Isaiah 28:19b, he says, 'For only *Anfechtung* teaches us to tend to the word.' " Klaus Schwarzwäller, *Cross and Resurrection: God's Wonder and Mystery*, trans. Mark Mattes and Ken Sundet Jones (Minneapolis: Fortress Press, 2012), 99.

8 Martin Brecht, *Martin Luther: The Preservation of the Church 1532–1546* (Minneapolis: Fortress Press, 1993), 14.

without ceasing" and meditate on God's Word day and night in accordance with Psalm 1.

Luther knows that the flesh and the devil always attempt to impede the discipline of prayer, so he writes, "When I feel that I have become cool and joyless in prayer because of other thoughts (for the flesh and the devil always impede or obstruct prayer), I take my little psalter, hurry to my room, or, if it be the day and hour for it, to church where a congregation is assembled and, as time permits, I say quietly to myself and word-for-word the Ten Commandments, the Creed, and if I have time, some words of Christ or of Paul, or some psalms, just as a child might do" (AE 43:193). While Luther offers Peter a number of pragmatic suggestions regarding the time and place of prayer, his focus is on the Lord's Prayer, the Ten Commandments, and, to a lesser extent, the Creed.

Luther gives a "model prayer" that serves as a preface to the Lord's Prayer. This prayer begins with a confession of unworthiness on account of sin, grounds prayer in the command and promise of God—echoing the Small Catechism—and implores the Father in the name of Jesus and in communion with "all thy saints and Christians on earth" (AE 43:194–95). Each petition of Jesus' prayer is used as a foundation and platform for praying. Luther shows Peter how to unpack each petition for supplication and intercession. He provides model prayers as well as pastoral instruction along the way. For example, Luther inserts parenthetical admonition in regard to the person unable to forgive his neighbor under the Fifth Petition.

The great word of prayer is "Amen." It is the word of faith that binds us together with all Christians: "Finally, mark this, that you must always speak the Amen firmly. Never doubt that God in his mercy will surely hear you and say 'yes' to your prayers. Never think that you are kneeling or standing alone, rather think that the whole of Christendom, all devout Christians, are standing there beside you and you are standing among them in a common, united petition which God cannot disdain. Do not leave your prayer without having said or thought, 'Very well, God has heard my prayer; this I know as a certainty and a truth.' That is what Amen means" (AE 43:198).

Praying the Lord's Prayer does not bind us to "words or syllables" but focuses attention on the thoughts comprehended therein. "It may happen occasionally that I may get lost among so many ideas in one petition that I forgo the other six. If such an abundance of good thoughts comes to us we ought to disregard the other petitions, make room for such thoughts, listen in silence, and under no circumstances obstruct them. The Holy Spirit himself preaches here, and one word of his sermon is far better than a thousand of our prayers. Many times I have learned more from one prayer than I might have learned from much reading and speculation" (AE 43:198). Just as a barber has to pay attention to how he uses his razor, so must the Christian attend to prayer with "concentration and singleness of heart" (AE 43:199). Luther concludes, "This in short is the way I use the Lord's Prayer when I pray it. To this day I suckle at the Lord's Prayer like a child, and as an old man eat and drink from it and never get my fill. It is the very best prayer, even better than the psalter, which is so very dear to me. It is surely evident that a real master composed and taught it. What a great pity that the prayer of such a master is prattled and chattered so irreverently all over the world! . . . In a word, the Lord's Prayer is the greatest martyr on earth (as are the name and word of God). Everybody tortures and abuses it; few take comfort and joy in its proper use" (AE 43:200).

Reinhard Huetter has written of the "Lutheran eclipse" of the Ten Commandments as a text for prayer and worship.[9] Such a disappearance is not due to Luther.[10] Like the Lord's Prayer, the Ten Commandments are to be prayed. Luther suggests a fourfold template for praying the Ten Commandments: "I take one part after another and free myself as much as possible from distractions in order to pray. I divide each commandment into four parts, thereby fashioning a garland of four strands. That is, I think of each commandment as, first, instruction, which is really what it is intended to be, and consider what the Lord God demands of me so earnestly. Second, I turn it into a thanksgiving; third, a confession; and fourth, a prayer" (AE 43:200).

Luther then provides model prayers. For example, with the First Commandment, Luther sees these four parts: (a) instruction—God teaches and expects us to have faith in no one or nothing other than God Himself; (b) thanksgiving—God is our God, and He has provided us with all that we are and all that we have; (c) confession—we acknowledge our "countless acts of idolatry" and our ingratitude; and (d) prayer—preserve us from unbelief and ingratitude. In this way, Luther sees the Decalogue as providing multiple dimensions for prayer. He writes, "'These are the Ten Commandments in their fourfold aspect, namely, as a school text, song book, penitential book, and prayer book. They are intended to help the heart come to itself and grow zealous in prayer" (AE 43:209).

---

9 Reinhard Huetter, "The Ten Commandments as a Mirror of Sin(s): Anglican Decline—Lutheran Eclipse," *Pro Ecclesia* (Winter 2005): 46–57.

10 See, for example, Luther's catechetical use of the Decalogue in the German Mass (AE 53:63–64). For the use of the catechism in Reformation orders, see Charles Arand, "Catechismal Services: A Bridge Between Evangelism and Assimilation," *Concordia Journal* (July 1997): 177–200.

Luther concludes his instructions for Peter with "A Simple Exercise for Contemplating the Creed." Noting that the division of the Creed corresponds to the three persons of the Godhead, Luther invites Peter to consider each article in light of God's work and our need. So we ponder the magnitude of God's gifts in creation, redemption, and sanctification while lamenting our lack of faith and gratitude.

Luther's *A Simple Way to Pray* would become something of a devotional classic since it demonstrated the application of Reformation theology to the life of the laity by providing an evangelical discipline for prayer and meditation shaped by common catechetical texts. William Russell writes, "This document represents Luther's mature catechetical piety, the integration of theology and prayer in the context of catechesis. He shows here his long-standing attention to the practical concerns of the Christian life. His response to the question of his barber shows how the reformer viewed this kind of Reformation—believers living at the nexus of the Word of God, catechesis, and prayer. As a confessor of the faith, Luther recommends that believers 'pray' the chief articles of the church's confession, that is 'the Lay Bible,' as found in the catechism."[11]

Prayer is taught so that the believer will be armed for the battles of the life of faith. Prayer arises out of the crucible of life under the cross. In prayer, the believer lays hold of the promises of God even when contradicted by experience. Luther understands the Lord's Prayer as the cry of faith, a continuing lesson in the theology of the cross.[12] Grounded in God's command and promise, prayer emerges out of God's Word and finds its surety not in the security of the flesh but the certainty of faith.

11 William Russell, *Praying for Reform: Martin Luther, Prayer and the Christian Life* (Minneapolis: Fortress Press, 2005), 71.

12 For more on this, see James A. Nestingen, "The Lord's Prayer in Luther's Catechisms," *Word & World* (Winter 2002): 36–48.

CHAPTER 4

Pastoral Care in Light of Vocation

The Calling to Freedom

For Luther, the Christian's calling in the world, his or her vocation, is the arena for spiritual sacrifices. Spiritual sacrifices are rendered in the bodily life of the believer as his life is a channel of God's love and care for the neighbor in need. These sacrifices do not merit salvation or make a person righteous but express love for the neighbor. God does not need our good works, but the neighbor does need our works. Freed from the notion that he must make himself good in order to earn eternal life, the Christian is directed toward the neighbor's well-being. In *The Freedom of a Christian*, Luther writes, "Although the Christian is thus free from all works, he ought in this liberty to empty himself, take upon himself the form of a servant, be made in the likeness of men, be found in human form, and to serve, help and in every way deal with his neighbor as he sees that God through Christ has dealt and still deals with him" (AE 31:366).

Here the Christian is the *larvae dei*, the mask of God, by which God gives daily bread to the inhabitants of the world. In this sense, the Christian is a "little Christ" to his neighbor. Again in *The Freedom of a Christian*, Luther writes, "Just as our neighbor is in need and lacks that in which we abound, so we were in need before God and lacked his mercy. Hence, as our heavenly Father has in Christ freely come to our aid, we also ought freely to help our neighbor through our body and its works, and each one become as it were a Christ to the other that we may be Christ to one another" (AE 31:367–68). Just as Christ sacrificed Himself for us on the cross, we give ourselves sacrificially to the neighbor in love. Luther expresses this in the seventh of his Invocavit Sermons preached at Wittenberg on March 15, 1522: "We shall now speak of the fruit of this sacrament, which is love; that is, that we should treat our neighbor as God has treated us. Now that we have received from God nothing but love and favor, for Christ has pledged and given us his righteousness and everything he has; he has poured out upon us all his treasures, which no man can measure and no angel can understand or fathom, for God is a glowing furnace of love, reaching even from the earth to the heavens. Love, I say, is a fruit of the sacrament" (AE 51:95). In his 1530 treatise *Admonition Concerning the Sacrament*, Luther makes a similar point: "Where such faith is thus continually refreshed and renewed, there the heart is also at the same time refreshed anew in its love of the neighbor and is made strong and equipped to do all good works and to resist sin and all temptations of the devil. Since faith cannot be idle, it must demonstrate the fruits of love by doing good and avoiding evil" (AE 38:126).

Holy Orders in the World

Luther's teaching on the dual existence of the Christian in faith and love leads us to observe a connection with the teaching of the two governments or two kingdoms. Leif Grane points out that for Luther "the place where the two kingdoms are held together is the calling."[1] This calling is lived within the structures of creation. Luther identified these structures as the three "hierarchies" of "the ministry, marriage, and government."[2] It is within these structures of congregation, political order, and family life (which for Luther included the economic realm) that one exercises "the liturgy after the liturgy." The Christian does not seek to escape or withdraw from the world as in monasticism, but rather he lives out his calling in the particular place where God has located him.

In his "Table of Duties" included in the Small Catechism, Luther identifies these duties as "holy orders" in an obvious play on words over against monastic teaching. Holy people do holy work. Sacrifice is relocated. No doubt Ernst Käsemann was influenced by the older liberalism that pitted "priestly religion" against "prophetic religion," nevertheless, he does echo a Lutheran theme in his exposition of Romans 12 as he states, "Christian worship does not consist of what is practiced at sacred sites, at sacred times, and with sacred acts (Schlatter). It is the offering of bodily

---

1 Leif Grane, *The Augsburg Confession: A Commentary*, trans. John Rasmussen (Minneapolis: Augsburg Publishing House, 1987), 174.

2 On the significance of the three hierarchies or three orders, see Oswald Bayer, "Nature and Institution: Luther's Doctrine of the Three Orders," *Lutheran Quarterly* XII (Summer 1998): 125–60, and Knut Alfsvag, "Christians in Society: Luther's Teaching on the Two Kingdoms and the Three Estates Today," *Logia* XIV (Reformation 2005): 15–20.

existence in the otherwise profane sphere."[3] In a less polemic tone, Carter Lindberg makes a similar point: "Daily work is a form of worship within the world (*weltlicher Gottesdienst*) through service to the neighbor."[4] The "thank, praise, serve, and obey" in the conclusion of the Explanation of the First Article find their fulfillment in the daily prayers and Table of Duties. The doctrine of vocation guides Luther's pastoral care of Christians living within these orders that are both holy and worldly.

Pastoral Care for Those Whose Callings Place Them in Danger

Luther provides pastoral care to those who live within their respective callings within the world. An example of such pastoral care can be seen in Luther's letter to John Hess of November 1527 where Luther responds to the Breslau pastor's question of whether or not one may flee in a time of plague. Just a few months before in the summer of 1527, the plague struck Wittenberg. The university was relocated to Jena where it would remain until the following April. Although the Elector ordered Luther and his family to leave Wittenberg in August, he refused to do so. Instead he continued lecturing on 1 John to the students who chose to remain in the town. Along with Georg Rörer, Johannes Bugenhagen, and Johannes Mantel, Luther would minister to the sick, dying, and grieving. Things would get worse in the autumn. Rörer's wife, Hanna, and newborn child would die on November 2 in the Bugenhagen home. Also, Karlstadt's

3 Ernst Käsemann, *Commentary on Romans* (Grand Rapids: Eerdmans, 1980), 329. Also note the comment of Paul Rorem, "Forgiven and renewed, we offer ourselves once again to God, not in mystery and ritual at the altar but in the gritty realities of the poor and the mission fields of our neighborhoods and work places." Paul Rorem, "The End of All Offertory Processions," *Dialog* (Fall 1996): 249. Luther speaks in the same way when, in a 1527 letter to John Hess, he describes how Christians are to go to the aid of the sick: "I know for certain that this work is pleasing to God and all angels when I do it in obedience to his will and as a divine service. . . . Godliness is nothing but divine service, and divine service is service to one's neighbor." Tappert, pp. 238–39. Also note the remarks of Carl Wisloff: "We, not the Sacrament, are the sacrifice. But we live from the gifts of God's grace, that is, we are led through them from death to life. Sacrifice finds expression in just this. This event finds expression in worship through thanksgiving, praise, creed, and witness. But a true sacrifice is only this when it is consecrated through faith by daily walking in baptism, that is, walking in fear and faith, death and resurrection." Carl Wisloff, "Worship and Sacrifice" in *The Unity of the Church: A Symposium*, ed. Vilmos Vatja (Rock Island, IL: Augustana Book Concern, 1957), 164–65. Also Oswald Bayer: "Worship is first and last God's service to us, his sacrifice which took place for us, which he bestows in specific worship—'take and eat! I am here for you' (cf. 1 Cor. 11:24 with Gen. 2:16). This feature of worship is lost if we want to do as a work what we may receive as a gift." Oswald Bayer, "Worship and Theology" in *Worship and Ethics: Lutherans and Anglicans in Dialogue* (New York: Walther de Gruyter, 1996), 154.

4 Carter Lindberg, *Beyond Charity: Reformation Initiatives for the Poor* (Minneapolis: Fortress Press, 1993), 108.

seriously ill sister-in-law, Maragret von Mochau, was staying with the Luthers at this time. Katie was pregnant with Elizabeth. Luther's son Hans was seriously ill. Luther referred to his home as a hospital. At the end of December after the epidemic had abated, Luther described his situation as hanging on to Christ by a thread even as Satan had bound him with an anchor chain and pulled him into the depths.[5] It was against this backdrop that Luther answered Pastor Hess's inquiry.

Luther provides an answer from the context of Christian freedom as it is to be applied within one's calling where both the offices of faith and love are exercised. Faith trusts in God's providential care in the face of danger, recognizing that one's life is in God's hands whether one stays or leaves. Believers are to commend themselves into God's keeping, whatever course of action they may take. So Luther writes, "If anyone is bound to remain in peril of death in order to serve his neighbor, let him commit himself to God's keeping and say: 'Lord, I am in thy hands. Thou hast obligated me to serve here. Thy will be done, for I am thy poor creature. Thou canst slay or preserve me here as well as if I were duty bound to suffer fire, water, thirst, or some other danger.' On the other hand, if anyone is not bound to serve his neighbor and is in a position to flee, let him also commit himself to God's keeping and say: 'Dear God, I am weak and afraid; I am therefore fleeing from this evil and am doing all that I can to defend myself against it. Nevertheless, I am in thy hands, whether in this or some other evil that may befall me. Thy will be done. My flight will not save me, for evils and misfortunes will assail me everywhere and the devil, who is a murderer from the beginning and tries to commit murder and cause misfortune everywhere, does not sleep or take a holiday' " (Tappert, pp. 235–36).

Luther acknowledges that some insist that the believer must not flee a deadly epidemic but accept the affliction as God's judgment and endure whatever fate may come in patience and unswerving faith while other believers think it acceptable to leave if not bound by other obligations. He also cautions that neither alternative is the grounds for inflicting the conscience of those who come to opposing conclusions. Those strong in faith may indeed wait the pestilence out, but they are not to bind those whose faith is weak to their opinion. "Let him who is strong in faith stay, but let him not condemn those who flee" (Tappert, p. 235).

However one may not flee an infected place if his calling to serve the neighbor is jeopardized. In cases where one's office—that of a pastor, governmental official, or medical worker—obligates them to serve the

5 See Brecht, *Martin Luther: Shaping and Defining the Reformation 1521–1532* (Minneapolis: Fortress Press, 1993), 209.

suffering neighbor, then there it is not a question in Luther's mind. They must stay even at the risk of their health and life in order to discharge their duty to the neighbor. Drawing on Christ's words in John's Gospel (10:11–12) about the hireling who forsakes the flock when the thief comes, Luther concludes that faithful shepherds will not forsake those committed to their care in order to save their own lives. Here Luther observes that there are two ways of fleeing death. One is to act contrary to God's Word or to recant one's confession of faith in order to preserve one's own life. The other ungodly way of escaping death is to abandon the neighbor in order to save oneself.

This does not mean for Luther that the instinct to preserve one's life is intrinsically wrong. He notes examples of Old Testament patriarchs and prophets who fled from death without abandoning their offices. Further, Luther suggests that if an adequate ministry is provided, not all pastors need remain in a time of crisis. Luther recalls the example of the apostle Paul in Damascus (Acts 19:30) who slips out of the city to escape persecution. Given the fact that other ministers remained in Damascus to provide spiritual care for the Christians there, Paul was not himself bound to remain and face unnecessary danger. In a matter of fact manner, Luther offers the counsel that "in time of death one is especially in need of the ministry which can strengthen and comfort one's conscience with God's Word and Sacrament in order to overcome death with faith. However, where enough preachers are available and they come to agreement among themselves that some of their number should move away because there is no necessity for their remaining in such danger, I do not count it a sin because an adequate ministry is provided, and, if need be, these would be ready and willing to stay" (Tappert, p. 232).

Luther does not call for impulsive heroism when the neighbor's well-being is not at stake: "The instinct to flee death and save one's life is implanted by God and is not forbidden, provided it is not opposed to God and the neighbor" (Tappert, p. 233). However, to neglect the well-being of the neighbor in body or soul is sin. Not only pastors but also those who hold secular offices necessary to protect the common good are bound to stay at their posts. Drawing on God's institution of governing authorities (Romans 13:6) and parenthood (1 Timothy 5:8), Luther notes that these responsibilities override personal comfort and safety: "No one may forsake his neighbor when he is in trouble. Everybody is under obligation to help and support his neighbor as he would himself like to be helped" (Tappert, p. 233). Since he had recently lectured to his university students on 1 John, Luther cites 1 John 1:14–17, where the apostle teaches that failure to love amounts to murder, to instruct his readers what is at stake here. The Fifth Commandment binds us to care for the neighbor, helping and supporting him in every physical need. "Godliness," Luther says, is "nothing but divine service, and divine service is service to one's neighbor" (Tappert, p. 239).[6] Christ hides behind the mask of the sick and needy to receive this service from us. To run away from an infected neighbor is to run away from Christ Himself.

Luther's letter to Pastor Hess expresses the place of faith and love in relationship to vocation. Faith that trusts in Christ alone is driven neither by foolish impulsiveness nor cowardice but by the confidence that, living or dying, our lives are in the Lord's hands. The language of Luther's morning and evening prayers is expressed in the realization that God gives His holy angels charge over us. They watch over us in times of danger and protect us in ways that exceed our imagination. Love will risk all things—even life itself—to do good to the neighbor in need. In the context of his particular vocation, the Christian is called to act with discernment.

Pastoral Care for Soldiers

The question of military service, which requires bearing arms with the possibility of killing, was not a theoretical topic for discussion. It appears that Luther's treatise of 1526 *Whether Soldiers, Too, Can Be Saved* was occasioned by Luther's conversation with a professional soldier, Assa von Kramm, who was troubled in conscience over the seeming conflict between his Christian confession and his profession.[7] Luther speaks to von Kramm as a pastor seeking to bring consolation and not as a military ethicist.

Fundamental to Luther's pastoral approach to the knight is the distinction between an occupation or office and the person who holds it. "In the first place, we must distinguish between an occupation and the man who holds it, between a work and the man who does it. An occupation or a work can be good or right in itself and yet be bad or wrong if the man who does the work is evil or wrong or does not do his work properly" (AE 46:94). Luther affirms that offices requiring the use of force, such as that of a soldier, judge, or executioner are legitimate; they are expressions of the divine authority attested to in Romans 13. Here Luther references his reader to his earlier book, *Temporal Authority: To What Extent It Should Be*

6 For a helpful discussion of Luther's understanding of the positive demand of the Fifth Commandment, See Albrecht Peters, Commentary on *Luther's Catechisms: Ten Commandments* (St. Louis: Concordia, 2009), 226–32.

7 See Brecht, *Martin Luther: Shaping and Defining the Reformation 1521–1532*, 342.

Obeyed, written a few years earlier in 1523 (see AE 45:75–129). The office of soldier is in and of itself right, but the person who stands in this office can misuse or abuse it. Such mishandling of the office is sin, but the sinful use of the office does not undercut the office itself.

Luther cuts to the chase as he identifies the crucial issue in light of the doctrine of God's justification of the ungodly by faith alone: "I am dealing here with such questions as these: whether the Christian faith, by which we are accounted righteous before God, is compatible with being a soldier, going to war, stabbing and killing, robbing and burning, as military law requires us to do to our enemies in wartime. Is this work sinful or unjust? Should it give us a bad conscience before God? Must a Christian only do good and love, and kill no one, nor do anyone any harm?" (AE 46:95). Luther argues that the Christian's righteousness is through faith in Christ and it is independent of any work or merit of the self. The soldier is not justified by the righteousness of his office but through faith alone.

The Christian soldier will exercise the office in faith and love. On the basis of Romans 13, Luther asserts: "For if it is wrong to use a sword in war, it also wrong to use a sword to punish evildoers or keep the peace" (AE 46:98). Accordingly, Matthew 5:39–42 cannot be used as a proof-text against Christians who are serving as soldiers. The Christian soldier does not finally put his trust in the rightness of his cause but in the righteousness of Christ alone.

Even though a just war appears to be an act of violent evil, it is, in fact, an expression of love. Luther uses the image of a surgeon seeking to save life by amputating a limb, which, if left in place, would bring certain death: "Now slaying and robbing do not seem to be works of love. A simple man therefore does not think it a Christian thing to do. In truth, however, even this is a work of love. For example, a good doctor sometimes finds so serious and terrible a sickness that he must amputate or destroy a hand, foot, ear, eye, to save the body . . . In the same way, when I think of a soldier fulfilling his office by punishing the wicked, killing the wicked, and creating so much misery, it seems an un-Christian work completely contrary to Christian love. But when I think of how it protects the good and keeps and preserves wife and child, house and farm, property, and honor and peace, then I see how precious and godly this work is; and I observe that it amputates a leg or a hand, so that the whole body may not perish. For if the sword were not on guard to preserve peace, everything in the world would be ruined because of lack of peace. Therefore, such a war is only a very brief lack of peace that prevents an everlasting and immeasurable lack of peace, a small misfortune that prevents a great misfortune" (AE 46:96).

So the Christian who serves as a soldier recognizes his office as instituted by God. Luther writes, "This is why God honors the sword so highly that he says he himself instituted it [Rom. 13:1] and does not want men to say or think that they have invented it or instituted it. For the hand that wields this sword and kills with it is not man's hand, but God's; and it is not man, but God, who hangs, tortures, beheads, kills, and fights. All these are God's works and judgments" (AE 46:96). To buttress his case, Luther cites Luke 3:14 where soldiers were coming to John the Baptist, and he notes that the Baptist does not call upon them to renounce the office and become pacifists, but to discharge their duties with integrity: "Thus he praised the military profession, but at the same time forbade its abuse" (AE 46:97). The occupation does not render the person righteous or unrighteous. Faith and unbelief do that. The one who is righteous through faith in Christ Jesus now lives within his earthly office with righteousness toward the neighbor. Righteousness toward the neighbor entails life in God's worldly government, which includes participation in the structures that the Creator has put in place to restrain and curb evil. In this way Luther counsels soldiers to understand their vocation in light of both faith and love, devoting themselves to their work with a clear conscience before God.

In the fear of God and with faith in the righteousness of Christ alone, the soldier is to receive the office of soldier while praying, "Dear Lord, you see that I have to go to war, though I would rather not. I do not trust, however, in the justice of my cause, but in your grace and mercy, for I know that if I were to rely on the justice of my cause and were confident because of it, you would rightly let me fall as one whose fall was just, because I relied upon my being right and not upon your sheer grace and kindness" (AE 46:123). The conscience of the Christian soldier must finally rest at the same place where the believer in every calling must find peace: the righteousness of Jesus Christ alone. All of our callings are the places where sin demonstrates its invasive power. None is righteous in himself. Our vocations continually drive us back to Christ and the forgiveness of sins in Him.

CHAPTER 5

Pastoral Care for Marriages

An Evangelical and Vocational Understanding of Marriage

Luther's understanding of marriage develops gradually, but it is firmly in place by 1523 two years before his own marriage to Katharina von Bora. In his *A Sermon on the Estate of Marriage* in 1519, Luther still regards marriage as a sacrament (AE 44:7–14).[1] The change is evident the next year in *The Babylonian Captivity of the Church* where marriage is divested of its sacramental status (AE 36:3–126). Carter Lindberg aptly describes the change in Luther's thinking and its implication for his pastoral work: "Luther's application of evangelical theology to marriage and family desacramentalized marriage; desacralized the clergy and resacralized the life of the laity; opposed the maze of canonical impediments to marriage; strove to unravel the skein of canon law, imperial law, and German customs; and joyfully affirmed God's good creation, including sexual relations. In return, Luther was in such demand as a marriage counselor that he often complained of the burden imposed on him."[2]

A cursory reading of the Small Catechism indicates that Luther treats marriage as a divine gift granted in the First Article, protected by the Fourth, Sixth, and Tenth Commandments, thankfully received as daily bread in the Fourth Petition, and lived out vocationally in the Table of

1 The scholarship on Luther's understanding of marriage is extensive. The most important treatments include Paul Althaus, *The Ethics of Martin Luther,* trans. Robert C. Schultz (Philadelphia: Fortress Press, 1972), 83–100; Oswald Bayer, "Luther's View of Marriage" in *Freedom in Response: Lutheran Ethics: Sources and Controversies* (Oxford: Oxford University Press, 2007), 169–82; Scott Hendrix, "Luther on Marriage," *Lutheran Quarterly* (Autumn 2000): 335–50; William Lazareth, "ELCA Lutherans and Luther on Heterosexual Marriage," *Lutheran Quarterly* (Autumn 1994): 235–68; William Lazareth, *Luther on the Christian Home* (Philadelphia: Muhlenberg Press, 1960); Carter Lindberg, "The Future of a Tradition: Luther and the Family" in *All Theology is Christology: Essays in Honor of David P. Scaer,* ed. Dean Wenthe et al. (Fort Wayne: Concordia Theological Seminary Press, 2000), 133–51; and James A. Nestingen, "Luther on Marriage, Vocation and the Cross," *Word & World* (Winter 2003): 31–39.

2 Carter Lindberg, "The Future of a Tradition," 133.

Duties. In his 1522 treatise on *The Estate of Marriage*, Luther notes his own reluctance at taking up the task of sorting out the tangled confusions created by abuses of the gift of marriage, yet pastoral necessity demands that he attends to marriage for the sake of bewildered consciences: "How I dread preaching on the estate of marriage! I am reluctant to do it because I am afraid if I once get involved in the subject it will make a lot of work for me and for others. The shameful confusion wrought by the accursed papal law has occasioned so much distress, and the law authority of both the spiritual and temporal swords has given rise to so many dreadful abuses and false situations, that I would much prefer neither to look into the matter nor hear of it. I must proceed. I must try to instruct poor bewildered consciences, and take up the matter boldly" (AE 45:17).

Grounded in Creation

Luther sees marriage as grounded in creation. In a marriage sermon from 1531, Luther says, "Who is there who does not know that marriage was founded and ordained by God, created in Paradise and confirmed and blessed outside Paradise?—just as Moses says in Gen. 1, 2 and 9. Everybody knows it. Even I learnt to recite the words. But really to hear and learn those words is such a skill that I still have not managed it. I'm still learning."[3] It is not a sacrament that bestows forgiveness, but there is no higher social calling where faith is exercised than that of the family. Marriage is the arena for faith and love. Hence the pope has no authority to impose vows that run counter to creation. Thus Luther condemned the clerical tyranny of marriage as well as the sexual chaos evident in fornication. "Setting bewildered consciences free and bringing them clarity and certainty cannot be accomplished by honing the fine points of the law and threatening punishments. What God says about marriage is a gift, not a law."[4]

Much of Luther's pastoral care in marriage matters was directed to those whose conscience was troubled by the vow to celibacy that they had made under the papacy. In a letter to his father, John, Luther addresses celibacy and marriage. Written in November 1521, the letter was intended less for Luther's father than for the monks, nuns, and priests who would read it. In this piece Luther sets in place basic components for an evangelical understanding of both virginity and marriage. Luther recalls how he resisted his father and took monastic vows: "For my vow was not worth a fig since by taking it I withdrew myself from the authority of my father and

3 Cited by Oswald Bayer in "Luther's View of Marriage," 171.

4 Bayer, "Luther's View of Marriage," 168.

the intent of God's commandment" (Tappert, p. 260). Luther recognizes that his monastic vow was not based on God's Word: "In short, it was taken in accordance with the doctrines of men and the superstition of hypocrites, which God has not commanded" (Tappert, p. 260).

Scripture does not exalt virginity over marriage. "In a word, although the Scriptures do not laud virginity, but only give it approval, these men, who are so ready to inflame men's souls for a life that endangers their salvation, dress it out in borrowed feathers by applying to it the praises that the Scriptures bestow on the purity of the married life" (Tappert, p. 261).

The Christian has the liberty of conscience that comes from being a new creature in Christ. Luther says that he does not belong to the cowl for the cowl belongs to him for all things are his in Christ. "My conscience is free, and this is the most complete liberty. Therefore, I am still a monk and yet not a monk. I am a new creature, not of the pope, but of Christ" (Tappert, p. 262). The Church has no authority over the Word and over the parental office. Luther says to his father: "On your side is the authority of God, on my side is human presumption" (Tappert, p. 260).

A few years later, in a letter dated March 27, 1525, to Wolfgang Reissenbusch occasioned by his hesitation to set aside the vow of celibacy, Luther restates his basic arguments against required celibacy, especially accenting the authority of Scripture and conscience. In this letter Luther reassures Reissenbusch that the renunciation of the vow is not sinful. Vows must be possible of fulfillment and within our ability to keep. God's creative Word cannot be restrained by vows or laws: "This is the Word of God, through whose power procreative seed is planted in man's body and a natural, ardent desire for woman is kindled and kept alive. This cannot be restrained either by vows or by laws. For it is God's Law and doing" (Tappert, p. 273). Men's bodies are formed from the flesh of women and so they seek union with women: "Our bodies are in great part the flesh of women, for by them we were conceived, developed, borne, and suckled, and nourished, and it is quite impossible to keep entirely apart from them. This is in accord with the Word of God. He has caused it to be so and wishes it so" (Tappert, p. 273). The vow to celibacy is against both God's Word and nature and is, therefore, "null and void" (Tappert, p. 273).[5] Luther says that such a vow is as foolish "as if somebody should vow to be God's mother or

5 Sammeli Juntunen notes that "the ideal of celibacy had led to widespread prostitution, openly practiced and tolerated not only by society but also by the church. If a priest could not adhere to the celibacy required of him, it was (at least in some parts of Europe) quite normal to use the services of a prostitute if the priest had paid a fine to the bishop. This was a lesser sin than to give up the priesthood altogether and marry." Juntunen, "Sex" in *Engaging Luther: A (New) Theological Assessment*, ed. Olli-Pekka Vainio (Eugene, OR: Cascade Books/Wipf & Stock, 2010), 187; used by permission of Wipf and Stock Publishers. www.wipfandstock.com.

make a heaven" (Tappert, p. 274). The vow is against the Christian faith in that it relies on works and not God's grace in Christ. "Of this sort are all monastic vows; they establish hearts and consciences on works and not on grace, and by this reliance on works men deny Christ and lose faith" (Tappert, p. 274).

God's Word establishes marriage in honor. It is the devil who shames and slanders marriage. To be ashamed of marriage is to be ashamed of being human. By such an attitude a man attempts "to make himself better than God made him" (Tappert, p. 275). Luther urges Reissenbusch to defy the devil and enter into marriage gladly.

On August 6, 1524, Luther wrote a letter to three unnamed nuns. This letter is representative of the advice that Luther often gave to monks and nuns concerning vows. Basically, Luther states that there are two grounds for abandoning the monastic life. The first would be when these vows are not voluntary but imposed by force. This would especially be the case with children who were made to enlist in a monastic order at such a young age that they were unaware of what they were pledging themselves to endure. A second ground would be the power of God-created desires implanted within our humanity pressing a person into sinful lust.

Luther's *Marriage Booklet* as Pastoral Care

Civil laws rightly govern marriage. This is reflected in Luther's *A Marriage Booklet for Simple Pastors* appended to the Small Catechism (K-W, p. 367). Here Luther writes, " 'So many lands, so many customs,' says the common proverb. For this reason, because weddings and the married estate are worldly affairs, it behooves those of us who are 'spirituals' [clergy] or ministers of the church in no way to order or direct anything regarding marriage, but instead to allow every city and land to continue their own customs that are now in use" (K-W, pp. 367–68). The liturgical structure of Luther's rite reflects the fact that marriage is a worldly order entered into by believers with a good conscience. The vows are legally binding; they are made at the church door and then the couple comes before the altar for the Word of God and prayer. Bayer notes, "The liturgy, with its petitions and thanksgiving, does not part company with civil marriage. Rather it penetrates it. The public transaction before the eyes of the witnesses, important in itself, is transformed by the fact that something else is given public expression at the same time: the fact that this relationship has not come about of itself. It has been given to us as a gift by God for which we are grateful: 'What do you have that you did not receive?' (1 Cor.

4:7). A Christian marriage service takes this into account and becomes a confession of our own poverty."[6]

Luther: The Marriage Counselor

In a Table Talk recorded by Jerome Weller in 1536, Luther complains about all the time that he spends working with troubled marriages. He wonders how Adam and Eve survived as husband and wife after the fall. "There is no doubt that during their long life they encountered numberless evils as they sighed over their Fall. It must have been an extraordinary regime! And so Genesis is a remarkable book of wisdom and reason" (Tappert, p. 283). A happy marriage is "a rare gift" (Tappert, p. 283). While enjoying a happy marriage to his own wife, Luther had to deal with marriages that were not so happy.

Stephen Roth seeks Luther's counsel regarding an appropriate course of action as his wife is unwilling to accompany him to Zwickau where he had received a new position. Luther's sarcasm shows up as he describes Mrs. Roth as "Your lord and mistress" (Tappert, p. 277). Luther faults Stephen for the wife's behavior, noting that he had been indulgent and submissive toward her. "Indeed, I am beginning to be somewhat put out with you too, for by your softheartedness you have turned into tyranny that Christian service which you owe her, and you have hitherto so encouraged her that it would seem to be your own fault that she now ventures to defy you in everything. Certainly when you saw that the fodder was making the ass insolent (that is, that your wife was becoming unmanageable as a result of your indulgence and submissiveness), you should have remembered that you ought to obey God rather than your wife, and so you should not have allowed her to despise and trample underfoot that authority of the husband which is the glory of God, as Saint Paul teaches. It is enough that you yield this glory of God to such an extent that you take on the form of a servant, but when it is done away, wiped out, and reduced to nothing, this is going too far" (Tappert, p. 277).

Luther then poses the diagnostic question. Is Mrs. Roth's refusal to move rooted in malice or infirmity? "Infirmity is to be borne; malice must be counteracted" (Tappert, p. 278). Luther concludes the letter by noting that Roth is an intelligent man and he will come to understand this pastoral counsel. Luther wishes that this couple "come to an agreement"

---

6 Oswald Bayer, "The Protestant Understanding of Marriage and Family" in *Freedom in Response: Lutheran Ethics: Sources and Controversies* (Oxford: Oxford University Press, 2007), 174.

so that Satan is driven off. The chief pastoral concern for Luther is that the devil might be prevented from using this marital dispute as an occasion for enticing the Roths into sin.

Difficult Cases

Nothing is known about the circumstances that brought forth the letter to Valentine Hausmann on January 27, 1538. It is apparent that Hausmann is seeking to separate from his wife on account of her behavior. Luther admits ignorance of all the details of this situation. He does remind his friend of the place of tribulation and cross in the Christian life. Hausmann is urged to remain faithful to his marriage and show mercy to his erring wife. He is not to seek an easy way out. He is to proceed by grace and not by the Law. “If you proceed strictly in terms of the law, much unhappiness may result and you may ultimately regret it, have a sense of guilt, and suffer heartache. Grace goes before the law, and too strict an adherence to the law will result in a loss of grace both in God’s sight and in man’s” (Tappert, p. 285).

Perhaps the most troublesome of the cases of Luther’s pastoral care in matters related to marriage is his counsel to Philip of Hesse, who was married to Christina, the daughter of Duke George of Albertine Saxony, in 1523. Philip was nineteen years old at the time of the marriage. Although he claimed “he never had any love or desire for her on account of her form, fragrance, and manner” (Tappert, p. 288), he fathered seven children with Christina. Through Martin Bucer, Philip contacted Luther and sought his endorsement in taking another wife. In what Luther thought was a private, pastoral piece of advice, Luther reluctantly concurred that a second marriage would be better than a scandalous divorce or open fornication. Philip of Hesse publicized Luther’s pastoral advice to defend his bigamy.

It seems that Luther sees Philip caught between two wrongs—divorce and bigamy. In light of the fact that God permitted the patriarchs to have multiple wives, Luther concludes that less damage would be done if Philip took a second wife secretly without divorcing Christina. Luther’s advice to Philip would be in keeping with a comment he made in 1520 in *The Babylonian Captivity of the Church*: “As to divorce, it is still a question for debate whether it is allowable. For my part I so greatly detest divorce that I should prefer bigamy to it; but whether it is allowable I do not venture to decide” (AE 36:105).

Luther thought that his advice was given under “the seal of the confession” and was the best that could be offered under the circumstances.

In defending his advice, he recalled the words of one of his teachers: "Alas, these cases are so confused and desperate that neither wisdom, law, nor reason can be of any help. They must be committed to God's mercy" (Tappert, p. 290). Luther was attempting to do the best that he could do when every solution seemed to be full of sin.

Where the Sixth Commandment was willfully broken and there was no indication of repentance, Luther did not refrain from practicing church discipline, binding the adulterer to his sin, as seen in his dealing with a Wittenberg city official, Joseph Levin Metzch. In a letter to Elector John of Saxony written on June 16, 1531, Luther complains about the scandalous life of Metzch who "was tied so tight to whores' pigtails that he shows few signs of fearing God" (Tappert, p. 280). Luther privately forbade him to receive the Sacrament. In a Table Talk recorded by Anthony Lauterbach on October 15, 1538, Luther addresses the ongoing problem of Metzch's fornication. Luther sent two deacons with the message that the absolution that Metzch received on the past Sunday was "null and void because he did not acknowledge his guilt" (Tappert, p. 281). As such, "he received the Sacrament in his sins, unrepentant. He must bear this burden himself, not I" (Tappert, p. 281). If he wishes to receive the Sacrament again, he "must first be reconciled with us preachers, pastors, the university, and the town" (Tappert, p. 282). Luther restates his ban on Metzch from the Sacrament and from serving as a baptismal sponsor. Luther notes that this is the second admonition according to Matthew 18:15.

Hardship in marriage was not an excuse to dissolve the permanent, single-flesh bond that God established in bringing a man and a woman together as husband and wife. Luther recognized that sinners living together in such closeness would be tempted to bitterness and the hardness of heart that refuses mutual and ongoing forgiveness.

In contrast to the twenty-first century, divorce was a rather rare practice in the sixteenth century. More common was simple abandonment. Questions of pastoral casuistry would arise as to whether and under what circumstances the deserted spouse could remarry. A letter to John Wickmann written on November 2, 1537, addresses the question of desertion in marriage. In the case presented to Luther, a man had deserted his wife and could not be located. Seven years had passed. Luther says if the man cannot be located, this should be announced from the pulpit and a public notice posted and that the woman is now free to marry another man if no evidence can be found that woman did wrong. "If, according to the testimony of neighbors, it appears that the woman is not to blame, let the pastor in Eisenberg post a public notice on the church door and do the same in your village, citing the man (or somebody else in his behalf) to appear within four weeks. If he does not appear, announce it from the pulpit that the deserter has not appeared and that the woman is therefore free to marry again. Thereupon you may unite her in marriage with another man in God's name" (Tappert, p. 284).

Lived under the cross, marriage would be an arena for the conflict between God and Satan as the evil one seeks to overturn what God has blessed. Luther's marriage rite, unlike modern rituals, included the strong and sturdy language of "the cross that God has placed upon this estate" (K-W, p. 370).[7] The cross puts an end to the romanticism that sees marriage as an instrument of self-fulfillment. But through the cross of Christ, Luther knows that all of human life, including marriage, is hallowed and received as a gift. Therefore he can preach in a wedding sermon of 1531: "God's word is actually inscribed on one's spouse. When a man looks at his wife as if she were the only woman on earth, and when a woman looks at her husband if he were the only man on earth; yes, if no king or queen, not even the sun itself sparkles any more brightly and lights up your eyes more than your own husband or wife, then right there you are face to face with God speaking. God promises to you your wife or husband, actually gives your spouse to you saying, 'This man shall be yours. I am pleased beyond measure! Creatures earthly and heavenly are jumping for joy.' For there is no jewelry more precious than God's Word; through it you come to regard your spouse as a gift of God and as long as you do that, you have no regrets."[8]

---

7 On this modern omission, see Bayer, "The Protestant Understanding of Marriage and Family," 167.

8 Cited by Scott Hendrix, "Luther on Marriage," *Lutheran Quarterly* (Autumn 2000): 335–50.

CHAPTER 6

Pastoral Care for the Poor, Needy, and Persecuted

Mercy Received and Given

Luther was a man who had received mercy, and, out of that reception of divine mercy, he knew how to show mercy to those in spiritual and bodily need. Mercy is a fruit of faith. In his 1526 treatise, *The Sacrament of the Body and Blood of Christ—Against the Fanatics*, Luther writes, "As [Christ] gives himself for us with his body and blood in order to redeem us from all misery, so we too are to give ourselves with might and main for our neighbor" (AE 36:352). The need of the neighbor is not an occasion to perform a "good work" that helps achieve salvation, rather such need becomes the arena where faith is self-forgetfully active in love. In the medieval world, the poor were seen as being in the world for the sake of the rich both economically and spiritually. From an economic standpoint, the poor provided labor that would benefit the rich. Spiritually, the poor provided the rich with the opportunity to give alms, a work that would assure blessing in the world to come. "Luther's doctrine of justification cut the nerve of this medieval ideology of poverty. Since salvation is a gift of God apart from human works, both poverty and almsgiving lose saving significance. By despiritualizing poverty, the reformers could recognize poverty in every form as a personal social evil to be combated. Justification by grace alone through faith alone effected a paradigm shift in the understanding of poverty and the poor. Poverty is no longer seen as the favored status of the Christian, but rather a social ill to be ameliorated even if it cannot be ultimately cured."[1]

1 Carter Lindberg, "Luther on Poverty," *Lutheran Quarterly* (Spring 2001): 89. Also see the excellent study by Carter Lindberg, *Beyond Charity: Reformation Initiatives for the Poor* (Minneapolis: Fortress Press, 1993), as well as his, "No Greater Service to God than Christian Love: Insights from Martin Luther," in *Social Ministry in the Lutheran Tradition*, ed. Foster R. McCurley (Minneapolis: Fortress Press, 2008), 50–68, and Samuel Torvend, *Luther and the Hungry Poor* (Minneapolis: Fortress Press, 2008).

Kindness and loving service rendered to the neighbor is never lost. Such service is, in fact, rendered to God. "What else is all our work to God—whether in the fields, in the garden, in the city, in the house, in war, or in government—but just such a child's performance, by which He wants to give His gifts in the fields, at home, and everywhere else? These are the masks of God, behind which He wants to remain concealed and do all things . . . We have the saying: 'God gives every good thing, but not just by waving a wand.' God gives all good gifts: but you must lend a hand and take the bull by the horns; that is, you must work and thus give God good cause and a mask," says Luther in his lectures on Psalm 147 (AE 14:114–115). So the Christian labors not for himself but for the well-being of the people that God has placed in his path. "The center of Luther's ethic of vocation is not self-sanctification, but the neighbors' needs."[2]

Luther sees greed as a sin that must be addressed by the pastor. Ricardo Willy Reith observes that Luther recognizes the linkage Paul makes between greed and idolatry in Ephesians 5:5. Thus, "faith, the true worship of God . . . is incompatible with greed. Greed should thus be understood as idolatry."[3] For Luther greed is a sin against both faith and love. The one who is greedy fails to trust in God's provisions for the future and, putting confidence in possessions instead, is possessed by them. At the same time, greed is a sin against love because it closes the heart and the hand to the need of the neighbor. Generosity, on the other hand, is an act of both faith and love for it grows out of God's gifts and it bestows out of what it has received from Him. Luther's attitude was expressed in an episode in his own life. "Once, when Luther was traveling to Jessen [a little town on the Black Elster River] to recuperate, along with Dr. Jonas, Veit Dietrich, and other table companions, though he himself did not have all that much, he gave alms to the poor there. Dr. Jonas followed his example, with the explanation: Who knows where God will provide the same for me another time! To which Luther replied with a laugh: As if your God has not provided it for you already."[4]

---

2 Carter Lindberg, "Luther's Struggle with Social-Ethical Issues" in *The Cambridge Companion to Martin Luther,* ed. Donald McKim (Cambridge: Cambridge University Press, 2003), 170.

3 Ricardo Willy Reith, "Luther on Greed" in *Harvesting Martin Luther's Reflections on Theology, Ethics, and the Church,* ed. Timothy J. Wengert (Grand Rapids: Eerdmans, 2004), 154. Also see Kathryn D'Arcy Blanchard, "If you do not do this you are not now a Christian: Martin Luther's Pastoral Teachings on Money," *Word & World* (Summer 2006): 299–309.

4 Bayer, *Martin Luther's Theology: A Contemporary Interpretation*, trans. Thomas Trapp (Grand Rapids: Eerdmans, 2008), 96.

Pastoral Advocacy

These fundamental aspects of Luther's theology would shape the way in which he would show mercy to the destitute. Often Luther's pastoral practice of mercy would be expressed in personal advocacy for particular people in challenging circumstances.

Luther wrote a letter to George Spalatin requesting that he intercede with Frederick the Wise on behalf of a fisherman who had unwittingly fished in waters reserved for the Elector. Luther does not ask that the man be let go unpunished but only that his punishment not destroy him financially. "I do not ask that he go unpunished, for there must always be respect for the power of government, but I ask that his punishment should not deprive him of his living. I should suggest that he be put in prison for several days or be made to live on bread and water for a week in order that it may be manifest that the purpose is to reform and not destroy the man" (Tappert, p. 171).

A letter to George Spalatin from April 10, 1523, intercedes for twelve nuns that Luther helped escape from a convent.[5] One of these nuns is Katherine von Bora, the woman that Luther would marry on June 13, 1525. Luther uses this letter to rage against the papal tyranny that imposed celibacy on these women. Luther notes that he will do what he can to locate the relatives of these women or secure husbands for them. Yet he is still in need of funds for their support as he laments: "The poor, who would willingly give, have nothing, and the rich either refuse to give or give so reluctantly that they may lose credit for the gift in God's sight and rob me of my time" (Tappert, p. 173).

Luther writes to King Frederick I of Denmark in September 1532 urging him to have compassion on Christian II, the king's cousin and now his political prisoner. He urges compassion and mercy following the example of Christ, who showed mercy on his enemies. Such mercy is a fruit of faith: "Therefore, my gracious Lord, let his work be a fruit of faith, a glorious thank offering to God, a comfort and refreshment to the prisoner, and a pleasure and delight to us all. Ultimately Your Majesty will be glad and will be thankful to yourself and all who gave such counsel, and Your Majesty will at length confess that you would have been heartily sorry if you acted otherwise" (Tappert, p. 178). Luther's plea was unsuccessful as Christian II remained in prison for the rest of his life.

---

5 For more on this episode see Martin Treu, "Katharina von Bora, the Woman at Luther's Side," *Lutheran Quarterly* (Summer 1999), 156–78.

A letter to Elector John of Saxony in October 1532 appeals on behalf of a family forced into exile from their home in Altenberg. Luther notes that the action of D. C. (presumably Dr. Christian Baier) was too drastic. He notes that the law on D. C.'s books or in his head "is not the only law there is, still less is it eternal law" (Tappert, p. 179). With an allusion to Matthew 7:1–5, he suggests that D. C. has enough beams to remove from his own eye. For Luther the law of love trumps a legalistic imposition of the civil code without consideration how it might harm a displaced family.

Luther addresses a letter to the Vice-Chancellor Francis Burkhard in the summer of 1536, imploring him to go to the defense of an old woman, a certain Mrs. Kreuzblinder, who was mentally disturbed. It would not be salutary for the prince to punish a woman who is insane, for "punishment will not improve her or make her more rational" (Tappert, p. 183). Instead Luther asserts, "Here is a case where mortals are bound to each other by a chain of misery. But mercy ought to break fetters" (Tappert, p. 183). Compassion is called for in these situations so rife with suffering.

The letter "To All Godly Christians and Friends" was written as an introduction and commendation for the foreigner Francis Megara in May 1538. Luther notes that Wittenberg enjoyed the reputation of being generous to those in need. Recalling examples from the Old and New Testament, Luther urges kindness for the stranger even though some gifts may be lost on the wicked. Citing biblical examples of foreigners finding a place of refuge among the people of Israel, Luther references the thankful Samaritan leper (Luke 17:15) and the centurion (Luke 7:9), both of whom "turned out better than many an Israelite" (Tappert, p. 183).

Luther did not have patience with peasants who resorted to violence in the so-called Peasants' War of 1524–1525. He feared that the revolt would be destructive of both the temporal and spiritual kingdoms, and so he counseled the princes to crush the uprising lest anarchy and chaos rule.[6] Yet in July 1525, Luther writes a letter to Albert, the Archbishop of Mainz, on behalf of a young man, Asmus Günthel of Eisleben. Günthel was arrested and imprisoned after he was alleged to have joined others in storming a barricade. Luther urges the archbishop to act with leniency toward this youthful offender: "It is not good for a lord to incite his subjects to displeasure, ill will, and hostility, and it is also foolish to do so. It is

6 See *Admonition to Peace*, AE 46:3–43; *Against the Robbing and Murdering Hordes of Peasants*, AE 46:45–55; and *An Open Letter on the Harsh Book Against the Peasants*, AE 46:63–85. For a good overview of Luther's reaction to the Peasants' War, see H. Bornkamm, *Luther in Mid-Career 1521–1530*, trans. E. Theodore Bachmann (Philadelphia: Fortress Press, 1983), 355–99; and Brecht, *Martin Luther: Shaping and Defining the Reformation 1521–1532* (Minneapolis: Fortress Press, 1993), 172–94.

right to show sternness when the people are seditious or when they are unmanageable and stubborn in the performance of their duties, but now that they are beaten down, they are a different people and deserve mercy along with punishment. Putting too much in a bag bursts it. Moderation is good in all things, and as Saint James says, 'mercy rejoiceth against judgment' " (Tappert, p. 175).

Empathy for the Persecuted and Imprisoned

The Reformation would provoke persecution from its opponents. Added to Luther's pastoral workload was the task of spiritual care for those suffering on account of their embrace of the evangelical confession. Jakob Spreng, the prior of the Augustinian monastery in Antwerp, defended Luther's teachings as early as 1519. Political conditions were not favorable for those who confessed the evangelical cause in the Netherlands. The Edict of Worms was strictly endorsed. Spreng and his successor, Henry von Zütphen, were both imprisoned and threatened with the death sentence. Under this threat, most of the Augustinian friars recanted their confession. Three young men did not: Lambert Thorn, Heinrich Voes, and Johann Esch. For reasons that are not clear, Thorn was not put to death but remained in prison until his death in 1528. Voes and Esch were burned at the stake in the marketplace in Brussels on July 1, 1523.

Their martyrdom prompted Luther's ballad "A New Song Here Shall Be Begun," which recounts the steadfast confession even unto death of these early Lutheran martyrs.[7] Luther's song along with his "open letter" aimed at persecuted Christians in the Netherlands in August 1523 served as instruments of consolation for those who were shocked by the burning of these two men. Luther extols the sacrifice of Voes and Esch because their martyrdom is not a sign of defeat but a manifestation of the victory of the Gospel: "Be of good cheer and rejoice in Christ, and let us thank him for the great signs and wonders that he has begun to do among us. He has given us a new and fresh illustration of his own life, and now it is time that the Kingdom of God should not be in word but in power" (Tappert, p. 193). Luther uses numerous biblical texts to remind readers of this letter that suffering for the Gospel is an honor that Christians bear because they have the sure and trustworthy promises of Christ, who alone is our joy.

---

7 For the text of the ballad, see AE 53:211–16. Also see Bornkamm, *Luther in Mid-Career 1521–1530*, 100–3; Brecht, *Martin Luther: Shaping and Defining the Reformation 1521–1532*, 102–4; and Robert Kolb, *Changing Perceptions of Martyrdom and Sainthood in the Lutheran Reformation* (Macon, GA: Mercer University Press, 1987), 21ff.

The theme of the Christians' persistent joy in persecution dominates the letter. Yet this is no giddy, self-made happiness that ignores or suppresses suffering and affliction; it is the deep reality that persecuted believers are one with their Lord. They share in His shame but also in His glory. Citing Psalm 116:15, Luther impresses on these grieving Christians the truth that the death of God's saints is precious in His eyes. Courage in the face of tribulation and gladness in the midst of sadness are no mere pious wishes or unattainable virtues for which to strive. They are reality for those who know that it is through dying we come to life. This is the bold comfort Luther gives to those who have experienced the tyranny of the evil one.

Luther did not forget Lambert Thorn, who was spared death for the moment. In January 1524, Luther writes Thorn an epistle of encouragement anticipating spiritual questions and struggles likely occupying the mind of this surviving prisoner. Perhaps Thorn wondered why his life was spared while his companions were taken. Luther addresses this possibility: "Who knows why the Lord was unwilling to have you die with the other two? Perhaps you were saved for another miracle" (Tappert, p. 198).

A striking and repetitive theme in this letter is the assertion that Christ is imprisoned with Thorn: "Christ, who is in you, has given me abundant testimony that you do not need my words, for he himself suffers in you and is glorified in you. He is taken captive in you and reigns in you. He is oppressed in you and triumphs in you" (Tappert, p. 198). In this letter we see the strength of Luther's Christology for pastoral care. The entire Christ, God and Man, is present with and for those who belong to Him by faith. The presence of Christ is not an abstraction for Luther. Christ is bodily present through His Word and according to His promise. No dungeon is too dark for His light, and no jail cell is so secure as to keep Him out. Erasmus detested the thought of Christ being present in the sewer (see AE 33:44–45). Luther knew that Christ is present with His Christians in agony and in death. Thus Luther can comfort the imprisoned Christian with knowledge that Christ is captive with him.

The loneliness of the dungeon could well be a fertile field for satanic temptation. As in other letters, Luther uses Holy Scripture to console and strengthen the suffering Christian in the face of temptation. In a potent paragraph, richly woven with biblical texts and images, Luther urges his friend to fix heart and mind on Christ: "And so, my brother, pray for me as I do for you, mindful that you are not suffering alone but that He is with you who says 'I will be with him in trouble; because he hath set his love upon me, therefore I will deliver him: I will set him on high because he hath known my name.' But all of us too are with you, as the Lord is, and neither he nor we will desert you. Be of good courage and he will strengthen your heart; wait on the Lord. He said: 'In the world ye shall have tribulation: but be of good cheer; I have overcome the world.' Do not argue with Satan but fix your eyes on the Lord, relying in simple faith on Jesus Christ, and know that by his blood we are saved. Just as our works and human laws cannot be the blood of Christ, so they can neither take away our sins nor justify us, can neither condemn nor accuse us" (Tappert, pp. 198–99).

With references to the Psalms, Philippians 1:6, and John 16:33, Luther comforts Thorn. The use of Philippians 1:6 and John 16:33 are common in Luther's consolatory writings and especially significant. Luther uses Philippians 1:6 ("And I am sure of this, that He who began a good work in you will bring it to completion at the day of Jesus Christ") to strengthen and assure those who suffer—an imprisoned confessor in this instance—that God's favor is not withdrawn. The good work that the Lord began in them by calling them to faith will not be dead ended or futile. It will come to eschatological fulfillment in the resurrection of the body at the day of the Lord's return. In the meantime, the Christian should endure in the confidence of John 16:33: "I have said these things to you, that in Me you may have peace. In the world you will have tribulation. But take heart; I have overcome the world."

As in other letters, Luther uses the Psalms to sustain Thorn, for in the Psalter the persecuted Christian is given words to pray that invoke God's deliverance, protection, and His final judgment of enemies. In this way the Psalter grounds lament in God's gracious promises. Oswald Bayer rightly reflects Luther's usage of the Psalms: "Although the full, uninterrupted praise of God's goodness, with which we praise God without affliction and temptation, will only happen at the end, the praise of God is nevertheless assumed in some way in every lament. . . . Lament directed to God is always related to some past and future praise."[8] Luther recalls what God has already done for Thorn in honoring him with an occasion to bear the cross and so give witness to the victory of Christ over His enemies, and then he uses the Psalms to testify to God's good and gracious will to bring that victory to perfection in "his day" (Tappert, p. 198).

8 Oswald Bayer, "Toward a Theology of Lament," in *Caritas Et Reformatio: Essays on Church and Society in Honor of Carter Lindberg*, ed. David Whitford (St. Louis: Concordia, 2002), 218.

CHAPTER 7

Pastoral Care for the Sick and the Dying

In the Shadow of Death: Sin and the Law

The late medieval period has been described as a time when life was dirty and cruel, brutish and short. The threat of disease and ever-present face of death were never far from the lives of Reformation-era people. Disease afflicts not only the body but also the soul and calls into question the goodness of God and His gracious purposes for sinners. "Originally death was not part of [man's] nature. He dies because he provoked God's wrath. Death is, in his case, the inevitable and deserved consequence of his sin and disobedience" (AE 13:94). Luther states the biblical truth (see Genesis 3:19, Psalm 90, 1 Samuel 2:6, and Romans 5:12–17). Death is the result of sin.

In his commentary on Psalm 118, Luther observed that "death always appears in the company of sin and the law" (AE 14:83). Bernhard Lohse describes this lethal companionship in Luther's thought: "Death, sin, and law are the terrible triad that always attacks us. Because Christians know of law and sin, they sense more strongly than others the horror of death."[1] Therefore Luther does not dismiss the terror of death as it confronts Christians but faces it head-on with the Gospel of Jesus Christ.

Luther lectured on Psalm 90 from late October 1534 to May 31, 1535. In these lectures he addresses the biblical understanding of death without

---

1 Bernhard Lohse, *Martin Luther's Theology: Its Historical and Systematic Development,* trans. Roy A. Harrisville (Minneapolis: Fortress Press, 1999), 331. Also note Werner Elert: "Under the Law the earthly way is the way of death and nothing else. The apostle's statement that the law of God is inscribed also into the hearts of the heathen is confirmed by nothing so much as the wisdom of the Greeks, which declares that the happiest man is he who was never born. Since he does not live, he need not die. To live means to have to die. But all of this is not the evangelical faith. Faith derived from the Gospel is faith against the Law, against appearances, against the God of wrath and of judgment, because it is faith in God's freedom, in the God of life, in the God who keeps His promises. This faith breaks every earthly hold and casts itself unreservedly into the arms of God." Werner Elert, *Last Things*, trans. Martin Bertram, ed. Rudolph F. Norden (St. Louis: Concordia, 1974), 15.

attempting to sanitize or sentimentalize death by cutting it free from sin, law, and divine wrath. No wonder Elert says of Luther's exposition of Psalm 90: "The basic total picture of man's existence is developed by Luther exhaustively but also with unparalleled gloom."[2] In Psalm 90, Luther sees Moses at the height of his power as a minister of the Law—*Mosissimus Moses*—"Moses at his most Mosaic" (AE 13:77).[3]

Here Moses magnifies death *coram Deo* so that sinners see death for what it is. The fall into sin is so pervasive, so deep, that man "does not even know his own sorry state, although he feels it and languishes under it. He neither understands its origins nor does he see its final outcome" (AE 13:76).[4] Instead Luther sees the human tendency to deny death or soften its irrevocable character. Complaining of theologians who engage in this evasion, Luther asserts that "following the example of pagan thinkers, they say in their funeral sermons that one should not grieve over death as if it were an evil; for death, so they assert, is a kind of haven, in which we are securely sheltered from the troubles and misfortunes to which the life of all men is subject. But this is the worst blindness and a further disaster—also a result of original sin—when we thus minimize sin and death, together with all other sorrows of the human race; when we thus oppose the universal judgment of mankind, yes, experience itself; and when we flatter ourselves with the most superficial and meaningless thoughts" (AE 13:76–77). Only by terrifying the secure sinner with the tyranny of death can the way be made clear for the proclamation of a genuine word of consolation in the promise of the resurrection. Luther refuses to see death as the result of human weakness or illness but as God's own verdict that He executes on the sinner.

Only when death is seen as a divinely wrought disaster can the broken sinner receive the comfort that God has placed in the Gospel. "The voice of the Law terrifies because it dins into the ears of smug sinners the theme: 'In the midst of earthly life, snares of death surround us' " (AE 13:83). Note here how Luther says that the psalm speaks to two kinds of sinners: the smug and the terrified and trembling: "Thus Moses suggests in the very

---

2 Werner Elert, *The Structure of Lutheranism*, trans. Walter Hansen (St. Louis: Concordia, 1962), 18.

3 Also see Brecht, *Martin Luther: The Preservation of the Church 1533–1546* (Minneapolis: Fortress Press, 1993), 156–71; and John A. Maxfield, *Luther's Lectures on Genesis and the Formation of Evangelical Identity* (Kirksville, MO: Truman State University Press, 2008), 19.

4 Also note Elert: "If sin were only disobedience, that is deviation from the norm, the damage could be repaired forthwith by obedience, and the problem of destiny would be solved by 'composure.' In reality, however, sin in the strict sense, is 'enmity against God,' that is active opposition to the will of God, which, to an equal degree, is active against sin. God replies to sin with a judgment that can only terminate in our death." Elert, *The Structure of Lutheranism*, 27.

title the remedy against the horrible doctrine of death and combines both—the remedy against, and the doctrine of, death—that those who as a result of this doctrine have been terrified and others might not become hardened and smug. These two factors must be joined, so that smug sinners and terrified and trembling sinners are cheered and encouraged, since they are told to follow the example of Moses, therefore, to believe and to pray" (AE 13:83). For Luther, ministry to the sick and dying will always be a ministry of both Law and Gospel. The Law is proclaimed to convict and condemn those who would shield themselves from the reality of death as God's judgment, while the Gospel is heralded to those who are terrorized by death on account of their sin. Luther sees Psalm 90 as tutoring the Christian pastor in this very work.

The approach of death challenges faith. Can God be trusted to bring His people safely through the dark valley of death into the bright vistas of the heavenly kingdom pictured in the Bible? Or is death the utter and absolute negation of God's promises? Death presses God's promises to the limits. Will they hold in that bitter hour when human senses fail and life itself slips away? These questions bear down on those to whom death draws near. Pastors are there to sustain Christ's people with His Word and Supper when they suffer bodily affliction that often touches the soul itself. With the rod and staff of their office, Christ's ministers should shepherd dying believers through shadows of death's domain, defending them against the devil's last and sometimes most fearsome assaults, into the security of Jesus' wounds. Luther does just this very thing.

Images for Consolation

Luther writes a dedicatory epistle to Elector Frederick of Saxony to accompany a devotional booklet Luther authored entitled *The Fourteen Consolations for Those Who Labor and Are Heavy-Laden.*[5] In this tract, written in 1519 and published the next year, Luther does several things. He observes that our Lord has given His Christians the mandate of caring for the neighbor in need due to sickness, suffering, or affliction. Works of mercy are part of the Christian life. This is known from both the word and example of Jesus. This obligation is toward all people but especially those of the household of faith as Paul says in Galatians 6:10.

5 The full text is available in AE 42:121–66. For helpful treatments of this work, see Neil R. Leroux, *Martin Luther as Comforter: Writings on Death,* 1–43; and Jane Strohl, "Luther's Fourteen Consolations," *Lutheran Quarterly* (Summer 1989): 169–82.

Christ Himself bears the sickness of the Christians. Therefore to minister to the needy Christian is to serve Christ, Luther maintains, on the basis of Matthew 25:40. Luther explains the evangelical and pastoral aim of his *Fourteen Consolations*. In contrast to the medieval legend of the fourteen saints who were seen as guardians against various evils, Luther draws from the Scripture fourteen descriptions of comfort that Christ gives the believer in the face of evil within and without. His fourteen consolations are modeled after a popular cult based on a legend from 1446 when a Franconian shepherd was said to have received a vision of the Christ Child accompanied by fourteen saints. It was claimed that each saint protected against a particular disease or calamity or served as a patron for certain groups of people. These images often served as the basis for altar paintings. Luther says that his images are not intended "to adorn the walls of churches but to uplift and strengthen the human heart" (AE 42:123). In this work, Luther sets seven evils and seven blessings together. Both evil and blessing are intermingled in this life. "The Holy Scriptures approach the matter of comfort in a twofold manner, insofar as they present to our view both blessings and evils, wholesomely intermingled. This is in accord with the word of the Preacher, 'In the day of evil be mindful of the good, and in the day of the good be mindful of the evil' (Ecclus. 11:25)" (AE 42:124).

Luther uses Romans 15:4 ("Whatever was written, was written for our instruction, so that through the patience and comfort of the Scriptures we might have hope") to show the source of Christian comfort (AE 42:124). Holy Scripture functions both to prepare the believer for suffering and to comfort in the midst of affliction: "It is thus very true that we shall find consolation only through the Scriptures, which in the days of evil call us to the contemplation of our blessing, either present or to come, and in the days of blessing, point us to the contemplation of evil" (AE 42:124).

Luther uses the template of fourteen images, seven of evil and seven of blessing, to help the Christian to recognize the complexity of evil that besets the Christian within this earthly life while also pointing the believer to the multifaceted nature of God's gracious work in Christ Jesus.

The First Image of Evil

The first image is "the evil within us." No torture can compare with the worst of all evils, "the evil within man himself." These evils within are far more comprehensive than we can apprehend: "The evils within him are more numerous and far greater than any which he feels. If a man were to feel his evil, he would feel hell, *for he has hell within himself*" (AE 42:125;

emphasis added). God chastises us with the knowledge of this evil, yet He shields us from the full impact of this evil: "As I have said, it is because God has so ordered things that man might not perish by seeing his innermost evils. God hides them and wants us to see them only by faith, when he points them out by the evil that is felt" (AE 42:126). Here Luther notes how deceptive this evil within us can be: "It is very true that we feel scarcely a thousandth part of our evils. And it is equally true that we measure, feel, or do not feel our evils not on the basis of the facts, but on the basis of our own thoughts and feelings" (AE 42:127).

The Second Image of Evil

From "the evil that is within us," Luther turns to a second image, "the future evil or the evil before us." Noting the uncertainty of what lies in the future, Luther counsels: "It will lighten your present evil in no small degree if you will turn your mind to the future evils. These are so numerous, so varied, so great, that they have given rise to one of the great and principal emotions, namely, fear. Fear has been defined by some as the emotion that is caused by a future evil" (AE 42:128).

Even if we are delivered from disease and other misfortune, death is sure to come for all. "Were it to be that possibly none of these evils should come, if it so pleased God, nevertheless, death, known as the greatest of all terrors, is certain to come" (AE 42:129). The certainty of death brings to mind our sin, for it is not our mortality that frightens us but the fact that we die as those who deserve death; we die as sinners.

Luther uses 1 Corinthians 10:12, "Let him who stands take heed that he does not fall," to remind his readers of the slippery path upon which we tread and the subtle power of the tempter who can destroy "us in a thousand different ways" (AE 42:129).

The Christian looks to death as deliverance from all evil. "The man who does not prefer the evil of death to the evil of sin loves God the Father but little. God has ordained that this evil be brought to an end by death, and that death can be the minister of life and righteousness" (AE 42:130). Death serves a salutary purpose when it brings to termination the evil existence in sin. For the believer, death spells the end of sin.

The Third Image of Evil

The third image that Luther focuses on is "the past evil, or the evil behind us." There is a special glory to this image for here "the sweet mercy of God the Father shines forth more brightly in this image than in the others and is able to comfort us in every distress" (AE 42:130). The past is a reminder of God's providential care. Luther uses biblical texts such as Proverbs 16:9; 1 Peter 5:7; Deuteronomy 32:10; Psalm 143:5; Psalm 77:11; Psalm 119:52; and Isaiah 54:7 to buttress his assertion that God's mercy and grace have surrounded us in ways that "we neither saw nor sensed" (AE 42:131). Knowledge of God's past guardianship and governance ought to prompt us to commend the present and the future into His care rather than be consumed with anxiety. God's kindness made manifest in His care in the past should give the Christian confidence to entrust whatever burdens the future may bring into His fatherly hands.

The Fourth Image of Evil

"The infernal evil or the evil beneath us" constitutes the fourth image of evil in Luther's sketch. There are two evils beneath us: death and hell. Death comes with condemnation empowered by the Law. Without the forgiveness of sins death is nothing other than the portal to hell. Every incidence of death ought to prompt us to repentance and faith. Hence Luther uses Luke 13:1–5 (Galileans whose blood Pilate mixed with their sacrifices; the eighteen crushed by the tower of Siloam) as an image of the death that we deserve on account of our sins. Such terrible happenings ought to prompt us to repentance rather than provoke speculation into the hiddenness of God that hardens the heart in unbelief.

The Fifth Image of Evil

The fifth image is "the evil on our left hand" or all those bodily afflictions that we suffer as victims of the purposes of wicked people. Luther observes that "the higher a man's position in life and the broader his rule, the more he is exposed to such persecution, intrigues, slander, and the plots of his enemies. In all of this we may again mark and feel the nearness of God's hand. Should we be surprised if now and then we are touched by one of these evils?" (AE 42:135). Both Christians and unbelievers suffer these afflictions. "However, their plight is worse than ours, because in a both bodily and spiritual sense they are outside of our fellowship. The evil that we endure is nothing compared to their estate, for they are in sin and unbelief, under the wrath of God and under the dominion of the devil, wretched slaves to ungodliness and sin. Even if the whole world were to heap curses on them, it could not wish them anything worse than what they have" (AE 42:135).

Misery can be borne by Christians because they are under God's favor and in His kingdom. "What God permits us to suffer is nothing compared to what they suffer. The reason these things affect us so little is that our hearts are not able to see how great is the shame and misery of a man lying in sin, that is, separated from God and possessed of the devil" (AE 42:136). On the other hand unbelievers have no consolation in their suffering for they are afflicted with an accusing conscience. Here Luther applies Isaiah 57:20–21: "The wicked are like the troubled sea when it cannot rest, whose waves cast up mire and dirt. There is no peace for the wicked, says the Lord God" (AE 42:136–37).

The Christian looks to the evil that afflicts his neighbor. "Christ was enkindled with such zeal and fervor when he died for us and descended into hell (1 Peter 3:19), leaving us an example that we should be concerned with the evils of others and completely forgetful of our own—no, covetous of our own" (AE 42:137). In this way the suffering of the neighbor is the call for the Christian to defend the neighbor and seek his bodily welfare.

The Sixth Image of Evil

The sixth image is "the evil on our right hand" or the evil that inflicts itself on those who are companions in the faith: "On the right hand are our friends, whose evil makes our own lighter, as St. Peter teaches in 1 Peter 5 [:9], saying 'Resist the devil in firm faith, knowing that the same sufferings are inflicted on your brethren in the world' " (AE 42:137). Luther cites Hebrews 12:4–11 to make the point that chastisement comes as discipline for our good. The Christian receives affliction also as a gift from the hand of the Father.

The trials endured by faithful Christians serve as examples for us. In the crucible of their affliction, there is temptation to be sure. Yet with temptation, God provides the way of escape (1 Corinthians 10:13). "Therefore, where there is greater evil, there is also more divine help and a way of escape, so that the inequality of suffering appears to be greater than it really is" (AE 42:139). Luther cites John the Baptist as an example of a man who died "as if unknown to God, man, and all creatures. Compared with such a death, what sufferings have we to boast of?" (AE 42:139).

Suffering is part of life in a fallen world. It comes in varying degrees to all. Echoing 1 Peter, Luther reminds his readers that their suffering should not be self-inflicted, that is, they should not suffer as evildoers but as those who faithfully confess God's truth. "Whenever you suffer, it is either because of your sins or your righteousness" (AE 42:140).

The Seventh Image of Evil

The seventh and final image of evil is "the supernal evil, or the evil above us." This is the evil of death itself, not merely the biological cessation of life but death as God's judgment on the sinner. Werner Elert reflects Luther's eschatological understanding of death when he writes, "Death does not intrude the field of ethics as a stranger who really belongs in biology, but he is at home here."[6] The venom of death is sin.

Christ Jesus has died our death by absorbing our sin into His body and suffering the fate of sinners under God's wrath on the cross. "There is nothing, not even death, that his passion cannot sweeten," writes Luther (AE 42:141). Suffering has been sanctified by Christ. "Surely, it comes to pass when you hear that Jesus Christ, God's Son, has by his most holy touch consecrated and hallowed all sufferings, even death itself, has blessed the curse, and has glorified shame and enriched poverty so that death is now the door to life, the curse a fount of blessing, and shame the mother of glory. How, then, can you be so hardhearted and ungrateful as not to long for and love all manner of sufferings now that these have been touched and bathed by Christ's pure and holy flesh and blood and thus have become holy, harmless, wholesome, blessed, and full of joy for you?" (AE 42:142).

Christians and unbelievers alike die. But for the believer, death is already an accomplished fact of his biography for he has died to sin in Baptism and now, the death that counts, the death to sin has already been died. "In death we are like all other men: the outward mode of our dying is not unlike that of others, except the thing itself is different, since for us death is dead. In like manner, all our sufferings are like the suffering of others, but only in appearance. In reality our sufferings are the beginning of our freedom as our death is the beginning of life" (AE 42:142). The sharp eyes of faith see even in temporal suffering the dawning of the new day when pain and suffering, sickness and death will be vanquished forever. Lohse captures Luther's eschatological outlook: "In Luther's doctrine death and the last judgment have fundamental significance: justification is of course received in the here and now, but it will be fully realized only in the hour of judgment before the eternal God. . . . Thus, for both his biography and theology, Luther's attitude toward death and judgment is the touchstone for truth and authenticity of everything said or written. A theology that does not reflect on the horizon of the end time misses both the truth of the gospel and the reality of human existence."[7]

In the meantime, the stance of faith is cross bearing. We embrace not relics but the suffering of Christ for us. "Oh, if we could only see the heart of Christ as he was suspended from the cross, anguishing to make death

6 Werner Elert, *The Christian Ethos,* trans. Carl J. Schlindler (Philadelphia: Fortress Press, 1957), 167.

7 Lohse, *Martin Luther's Theology,* 325.

contemptible and dead for us" (AE 42:143). In the midst of suffering, we are drawn to the One who was lifted up for the sins of the world. We look to Him alone and trust His promises as death approaches. Luther writes, "If we have learned from the preceding images, those beneath and near us, to bear our evils with patience, then surely this last image, in which we are lifted above and outside ourselves, caught up into Christ and placed beyond all evils, should teach us that we ought not only to tolerate these evils, but love them, desire them and seek them out. If such thinking is still foreign to a person, it means that the passion of Christ still has little meaning for him. This is evident in those who make the signs and arms of Christ to ward off evils and death, but are not ready to suffer or to die. This is altogether contrary to the cross and death of Christ. In keeping with this image we must therefore absorb and consume whatever evils we may have to bear, so that they will not only not grieve us, but will delight us. This will come true if this image finds its way to our heart and abides in the inner most affections of our mind" (AE 42:144).

The First Image of Blessing

Luther then sets the seven images of evil in contrast with seven images of blessing. The first image of blessing Luther calls the "blessing within us." Bodily gifts of health, strength, vitality, mental capability, and alertness are abundant gifts from God. "The enjoyment of these for a long or even a short season will soon teach us how we ought to conduct ourselves in the face of some small evil" (AE 42:145). The abundance of the blessings that Luther describes as daily bread in his exposition of the Lord's Prayer in the Small Catechism ought to evoke praise and thanksgiving rather than grumbling or complaint, for these undeserved gifts are a reminder that God's wisdom orders all things well. Luther references Job's confession, "If we receive good from the hand of God, why should we not also bear evil?" (Job 2:10), noting that "is a golden saying and a great comfort in the day of trial" (AE 42:146).

Bodily blessings are common to all, Christians and non-Christians alike. But the Christian has far greater blessings within—faith in Christ. "To have faith is to have the Word and truth of God, and to have the Word of God is to have God himself, the maker of all. If all these blessings in their fullness were revealed to the soul, it would in a moment break free from the body because of its exceeding abundance of sweet pleasure" (AE 42:147).

The Second Image of Blessing

The life of faith is eschatological, that is, Christian hope lives in the confident anticipation that God will fulfill His promises. So the second image of blessing is "the future blessings or the blessing before us." Luther draws a contrast between the believer and the unbeliever: "While in the midst of their evils, those who are not Christians will find but little comfort in contemplating future blessings, since for them all things are uncertain" (AE 42:148). The words of Jesus in Luke 12:16–21, the parable of the rich fool, illustrate an elusive and false hope in contrast to the certain hope that we are given in Christ. The Christian will also face death, but he does so as one who is in Christ in both life and death (Romans 14:8). Therefore, he can lie down to sleep in peace (Psalm 4:8).

God transforms the threat of death to a promise. "It is a great thing that death, which to others is the greatest of evils, is made the greatest gain for us. . . . It is indeed a divine work that he wrought, and it is not surprising that he made the evil of death into the greatest blessing" (AE 42:149). Christ has killed death by dying so that "for the believer death is thus already dead and behind its cloak and mask it holds no terror. Like a slain serpent, death still has its former terrifying appearance, but now this is only a mask, for it is now a dead and harmless evil" (AE 42:150). Luther makes a similar point in his Easter hymn written a few years later in 1524, "Christ Jesus Lay in Death's Strong Bands," where he confesses: "It was a strange and dreadful strife When life and death contended; The victory remained with life, The reign of death was ended. Holy Scripture plainly saith That death is swallowed up by death, Its sting is lost forever. Alleluia!" (*LSB* 458:4).

In this paradoxical way, death, which seeks to destroy, is now destroyed. Death, which entered as divine curse on account of mankind's sin, is now a blessing since it puts an end to all of life's punishments and sin itself. It delivers us from the perils of sinning. "Therefore, he who loves life and righteousness must not hate, but rather love, death, his servant and workshop, if he desires to attain either life or righteousness" (AE 42:151). God has "appointed death to be the destroyer of death." Paradoxically, sin is destroyed by its own fruit—death.

The Third Image of Blessing

The third image of blessing is "the past blessings, or the blessings behind us." As we reflect on our past, we see God's hand of blessing: "How very different our course would have been if we had been left to our own free will! Only now to do we understand God's ever-present care and providence over us, so that we were able neither to think nor speak anything except as he gave us leave" (AE 42:152). Luther cites Psalms 40:17 and 139:15–16 as testimony to God's care in the past. The Lord who formed us in the womb knows us better than we know ourselves. This God invites us to cast all our burdens and cares on Him (see Psalm 55:22; 1 Peter 4:19; 1 Peter 5:7). "If only a man could see God in such a light! How happy, how calm, how safe he would be! He would then truly have a God from whom he would know with certainty that all his fortunes—whatever they might be—had come to him and were still coming to him under the guidance of God's most gracious will" (AE 42:154).

The Fourth Image of Blessing

Luther turns to "the infernal blessing, or the blessing beneath us," the fourth image of blessing. How is it that the eternal torment of the wicked is a blessing? Luther answers, "Let us now look at the blessings that are found in others and which lie outside of us. The first is found in those who are beneath us, that is, in the dead and the damned. Isn't it strange that some kind of blessing can be found in them? However, the power of divine goodness is everywhere so great that it enables us to discern blessings even in the greatest evils . . . we see how immeasurable our gain is" (AE 42:155). We see in the damned the wrath of God from which we are delivered. This is not a rejoicing in the eschatological fate of the unbeliever but a reminder of the future that would have surely awaited us without faith in the redeeming work of Christ.

The Fifth Image of Blessing

The fifth image is "the blessing on our left hand." It is a good thing, Luther maintains, to see the temporal blessings that God has bestowed on the unjust. Luther uses Psalm 73 to make the case that the well-being of the wicked leads us to trust in God alone rather than envy. We are drawn to God, who clothes the flowers of the field and provides food for the birds (Matthew 6:26–30). This is the God who works all things for the good of His saints (Romans 8:28).

Luther raises the question: "What greater trial can there be than the host of evil examples?" (AE 42:159). Are not the faithful tempted to distrust in the purposes of God when they the wicked prosper in their evil ways while the righteous are afflicted? Yet God brings blessing and benefit out of trial and testing. "Thus it is good for us always to be oppressed with some trouble, lest in our weakness we succumb to the offenses of the world and fall into sin. . . . When the world is unable to swallow us up with its allurements or make us one with itself through its offenses, it endeavors by means of suffering to drive us out and by means of pain to cast us off. . . . For the end of the world, both of its pleasures and its tyranny, is poison and eternal death" (AE 42:159).

The Sixth Image of Blessing

"The blessings on our right hand" are the sixth image. These blessings are embodied in the brothers and sisters with whom Christ has placed us in His Church. We are not alone. "This is the communion of saints in which we glory. Whose heart will not be lifted up, even in the midst of great evils, when he believes the very truth, namely, that the blessings of all the saints are his blessings, and his evil is also theirs?" (AE 42:161). Here Luther cites Galatians 6:2 and 1 Corinthians 12:26 to demonstrate this bond. This bond is a real *communio*, or fellowship, for, to use Pauline language, we are one bread, one body together (see 1 Corinthians 10:16–17). The eyes of faith are opened to see that we are surrounded by the Church, the Body of Christ.[8]

The Seventh Image of Blessing

The seventh image is "the supernal blessing, or the blessing above us." This image is "Jesus Christ, the King of glory, rising from the dead, just as in his suffering, death, and burial he formed the seventh image of evils" (AE 42:163). Here the heart finds supreme joy and everlasting consolation, for Christ is raised from the dead never to die again. "Therefore, his resurrection and everything that he accomplished through it are mine" (AE 42:164). This theme is also echoed in Luther's Easter Sermon of 1544: "Thus we see another picture at Easter, that no sin, no curse, no disgrace, no death, but only life, grace, blessedness and righteousness are in Christ. With such a picture we should lift up our hearts. For it is put before us and presented in such a way, that we should receive nothing else than this, that God has himself awakened us today along with Christ. For just as you see sin, death and the curse in Christ, so you should also believe that God, for Christ's sake, will not see these in you, when you receive his resurrection

8 Here see also Luther's 1519, *The Blessed Sacrament of the Holy and True Body of Christ, and the Brotherhoods* in AE 35:49–73. In this treatise, Luther sees the Lord's Supper as a *communio*: "This fellowship consists in this, that all the spiritual possessions of Christ and his saints are shared with and become the common property of him who receives the sacrament" (AE 42:51). This motif recedes in the later writings of Luther on the Sacrament of the Altar. See Hans-Martin Barth, *The Theology of Martin Luther: A Critical Assessment* (Minneapolis: Fortress Press, 2013), 244.

for yourself and receive its consolation. Such grace faith brings to us. When that day will come, however, one will no longer believe, but see, touch and feel."[9]

Christ's resurrection bestows on us His righteousness and glory. He is "our most precious wagon," for we ride in His righteousness to heaven. Our Lord's righteousness and His life are now ours by faith. "That is to say, the law makes us sinners and sin makes us guilty of death. Who has conquered these two? Was it our righteousness? Was it our life? No, it was Jesus Christ, rising from death, condemning sin and death, imparting his righteousness to us, bestowing his merits on us, and holding his hand over us. Now all is well with us; we fulfill the law and vanquish sin and death. For all of this, let there be honor, praise, and thanksgiving to God forever and ever. Amen" (AE 42:165). Christ lifts us above sin, death, and every evil and seats us with Himself.

A Letter for the Journey

Vivid imagery like that in the *Fourteen Consolations* is often found in Luther's pastoral writing. It is seen on a more personal level in a letter Luther writes to his ailing father on February 15, 1530, just a few months before the elder Luther's death on May 29. This letter testifies to Luther's filial affection for his father and an affirmation of his father's faith in Jesus Christ. Luther gives thanks that his father has embraced the evangelical doctrine and has been delivered from the darkness of error. His father's faith is confirmed by the slander, mockery, and scorn he has borne for Christ's sake.

The son now writes to his father, urging him to let his heart be strong and take ease in this affliction for he has a true mediator with God, Jesus Christ. Admonishing his father to pray in the confidence of Christ's strong promises, Luther writes, "The whole Psalter is full of such comforting promises, especially Ps. 91, which is particularly good to read to the sick" (Tappert, p. 31).

Luther writes so that he might share in his father's faith, temptation, consolation, and thanksgiving. He writes with the recognition that in life and in death, the Christian belongs to the Lord. In words that echo Philippians 1:21–26, Luther reminds his father: "If it is his divine will that you should postpone that better life and continue to suffer with us in this troubled and unhappy vale of tears, to see and hear sorrow and help other

9 Cited in Gerald Krispin, "The Consolation of the Resurrection in Luther," *Lutheran Theological Review* (Fall/Winter 1989–1990): 44.

Christians to suffer and conquer, he will give you grace to accept all this willingly and obediently. This life, cursed by sin, is nothing but a vale of tears. The longer a man lives, the more sin and wickedness and plague and sorrow he sees and feels. Nor is there respite or cessation this side of the grave. Beyond is repose, and we can sleep in the rest Christ gives us until he comes again to wake us with joy. Amen" (Tappert, pp. 31–32).[10]

In this letter we note Luther's skillful use of concrete imagery in bringing consolation to his father. He compares death to a short journey: "Our departure from this life is a smaller thing to God than my journey from here to Mansfeld or yours from Mansfeld to Wittenberg. It is only an hour's sleep, and after that all will be different. This is most certainly true" (Tappert, p. 32). In this way, Luther is providing his own evangelically-centered *ars moriendi* (art of dying).[11]

Luther's Answer to the Purpose Driven Death

If Christians in the twenty-first century are fascinated by the "purpose driven life," their sixteenth century counterparts were taken by the *ars moriendi* as a kind of "purpose driven death." The Christian was to be armed with principles for dying in a purposeful way, not wasting the opportunity that chronic illness and aging bring. The Christian was to make amends for one's sin and engage in practices of penitential piety designed to make shorter the journey through purgatory to the heavenly city. Patience in physical suffering was thought to lessen the suffering that might be necessitated by the residue of sin in this mortal life. Fear of death was seen as natural since death represented entrance into a realm where God's verdict was uncertain at best and condemnatory at worst. The Lutheran Reformation represented a new understanding of death in light of both Law and Gospel. For Luther, the pastoral care of the dying would be marked by the forgiveness of sins for Christ's sake and, within that absolution, the sure and certain promise of the resurrection of the body

---

10 Werner Elert reflects Luther's thought in his description of what it means for the Christian to die in faith: "If I believe that God has created me, that He preserves my earthly life 'out of fatherly, divine, goodness and mercy,' as the catechism states, how could I then believe that this fatherly, divine, goodness and mercy suddenly ceases to operate when He lets me die? If physical death signified God's judgment *to* faith, it would also be His judgment *on* faith. If the apostle had conceived of it thus, how then could he have a veritable desire to 'depart' (*analysai*, Phil. 1:23)? No, physical death has lost its terrors for faith. Faith receives death from the hands of a merciful God exactly as it receives life. As has been said, 'Death has become my sleep.'" Elert, *Last Things*, 17–18.

11 For more on Luther's transformation of the old *ars moriendi*, see Austra Reinis, *Reforming the Art of Dying: The ars moriendi in the German Reformation 1519–1528* (Burlington, Vermont: Ashgate Publishing Company, 2007).

to life everlasting. "Fear of dying should be seen as a work of the devil and rejected."[12] Luther would provide an evangelical proposal for ministry to those nearing death.

Luther worked out this proposal in his 1519 *A Sermon on Preparing to Die*, a work that Gottfried Krodel called "an evangelical version of the popular late medieval *ars moriendi* books."[13] In this sermon, Luther compares a Christian facing death to an unborn child. After reminding his audience that people must take leave of this world both physically and spiritually, he admonishes them to direct their attention to God saying, "Since everyone must depart, we must turn our eyes to God, to whom the path of death leads and directs us. Hence we find the beginning of the narrow gates and the straight path to life (Matt. 7:14). All must joyfully venture forth on this path, for though the gate is quite narrow, the path is not long. Just as an infant is born with peril and pain from the small abode of its mother's womb into this immense heaven and earth, that is, into this world, so man departs this life through the narrow gate of death. And although the heavens and the earth in which we dwell at present seem large and wide to us, they are nevertheless much narrower and smaller than the mother's womb in comparison with the future heaven. Therefore, the death of the dear saints is called a new birth, and their feast day is known in Latin as *natale*, that is, the day of their birth. However, this narrow passage of death makes us think this life as expansive and the life beyond as confined. Therefore, we must believe this and learn a lesson from the physical birth of a child, as Christ declares, 'When a woman is in travail she has sorrow; but when she has recovered, she no longer remembers the anguish, since a child is born by her into the world' (John 16:21). So it is that in dying we must bear the anguish and know that a large mansion and joy will follow (John 14:2)" (AE 42:99–100). Martin Brecht observes: "Luther's Reformation theology had to pass the test of whether it was able to stand up to the last human fear."[14] With this sermon, the reformer demonstrated the potency of the evangelical theology to provide sure and substantial comfort to the dying.

Luther's mother, Margaret, would die a year after her husband. A little over a month before her death, Luther writes a letter of consolation to his

12 Brecht, *Martin Luther: Shaping and Defining the Reformation 1521–1532* (Minneapolis: Fortress Press, 1990), 208.

13 Gottfried Krodel, "Luther's Work on the Catechism in the Context of Late Medieval Catechetical Literature," *Concordia Journal* (October 1999): 398.

14 Cited in Neil R. Leroux, *Martin Luther as Comforter*, 46.

mother. In this letter Luther uses Romans 8:36 and John 16:33 to comfort her. He reminds his mother that the fatherly chastisement that we receive from God is ever so slight in comparison with the suffering of the godless. We have the confidence and comfort of Christ's victory over sin and death. Our God is not a severe judge or tyrant but a Savior and sweet Comforter. Luther anchors the consolation in the Means of Grace with a reference to Philippians 1:6: "To such knowledge, I say, God has graciously called you. In the gospel, in Baptism, and in the Sacrament (of the Altar) you possess his sign and seal of this vocation, and as long as you hear him addressing you in these, you will have no trouble or danger. Be of good cheer, then, and thank him joyfully for such great grace, for he who has begun a good work in you will perform it until the day of Jesus Christ" (Tappert, p. 36).

A Table Talk recorded by Conrad Cordatus in the autumn of 1531 gives us a glimpse into how Luther makes spiritual diagnosis and application of God's Word.[15] While attending to the man's condition, Luther moves to inquire of his faith. Pastoral conversation is never confined to a discussion of outward circumstances but finally must move to the heart of the matter, the condition of the sick person's trust in Christ Jesus.

A letter addressed to John Ruehel in June 1534 addresses the sick man's impatience. "The realization that you have been called by this Man, that you have been blessed by a knowledge, desire, and love for his Word, and that you have been sealed therein by his Baptism and Sacrament should surely make you more cheerful. What more do you expect of Him who has inwardly given you such love toward him and has outwardly given you such seals and such a confession and testimony of his grace? Dear doctor, behold the good things you possess at his hands rather than what you suffer. The balance is tipped immeasurably in favor of the former" (Tappert, pp. 37–38). In this correspondence, Luther preaches to Ruehel urging him to fix his attention on all that he has been given in Christ. The gift of the Lord's treasure surely outweighs the slight and momentary affliction that comes with sickness.

---

15 See Tappert, pp. 36–37 for the text of this Table Talk, which is actually more of a descriptive telling by Cordatus of how Luther approaches a sick man with gentleness inquiring of his infirmities and of his willingness to bear this affliction in patience and faith. When the patient replies that he is so disposed, Luther comforts him with the promise of God's mercy and admonishes him to steadfastness even as he assures him of his prayers. The man is grateful for Luther's visit. Cordatus records, "When the sick man begins to thank Luther and declares that he can never repay him for the blessing of his visit, Luther is accustomed to reply that this is his office and duty and that it is therefore not necessary to thank him so profusely. He also makes use of this consolation, that the sick man should not be afraid because God, who has provided him with a letter and seal (that is, with his Word and Sacrament), has also given himself for this man's redemption" (Tappert, p. 37).

Caspar Mueller was the chancellor of Mansfield and a friend of Luther. He served as a baptismal sponsor for one of Luther's children. In 1534 during an illness, Luther writes his friend and urges patient submission to the good and gracious will of the Father revealed in Christ Jesus. Christ bore for us the yoke of the devil and God's wrath and freed us from them. He now gives us the easy yoke and light burden. "This exchange is to be accepted cheerfully. He is a good merchant and a gracious tradesman who sells us life for death, righteousness for sin, and lays a momentary sickness or two upon us by way of interest and as a token that he sells more reasonably and borrows at more favorable rates than the Fuggers and tradesmen on earth" (Tappert, p. 39).

In this letter Luther uses a phrase from his hymn "A Mighty Fortress" to describe the Lord Jesus Christ as "the valiant man who fights for us" (Tappert, p. 39). As is often the case, Luther uses a memorable, brief phrase full of vivid imagery and spiritual potency to impress the Gospel on the heart and mind of one who is suffering. While sickness brings physical weakness and perhaps even spiritual turmoil, our confidence is in the stronger One who has plundered the devil's house and even now stands beside us as our refuge in every time of need.

The illness of Urbanus Rhegius,[16] a former Roman priest converted to the evangelical cause, provides Luther with an opportunity to speak of the place of trial in the life of the Christian. God uses affliction for our good. Sickness causes us to recognize our helplessness and drives us away from self. "By these vicissitudes he teaches us not to be arrogant, as we might be if we were always strong, and not to despair, as we might if we were always infirm. . . . We are best off when we ourselves acknowledge that we are framed of dust and are mere dust" (Tappert, p. 41). Pastoral care in times of illness is not an exercise in sentimentalities but a forthright speaking of and to the reality that human beings are not autonomous but creatures bound to the earth by birth and death.

Pastoral Care as Spiritual Warfare Against the Evil One

Sickness is not only a symptom of a world disordered by human sin and a reminder of the inescapable fact that death awaits all people; it is also tied

16 Rhegius (1489–1541) would carry forward the spiritual care he received from Luther in his own work. See, for example, Urban Rhegius, *Preaching the Reformation: The Homiletical Handbook of Urbanus Rhegius*, trans. and ed. Scott Hendrix (Milwaukee: Marquette University Press, 2003). Also see Ronald K. Rittgers, "Christianization Through Consolation: Urbanus Rhegius's *Soul-Medicine for the Healthy and Sick in These Dangerous Times* (1529)" in *The Reformation as Christianization*, eds. Anna Marie Johnson and John A. Maxfield (Tübingen: Mohr Siebeck, 2012), 321–45.

to the work of the devil himself. In the Large Catechism, Luther sees the wicked one as involved in the perpetuation of this disorder: "This petition ("But deliver us from evil") includes all the evil that may befall us under the devil's kingdom: poverty, disgrace, death, and, in short, all the tragic misery and heartache, of which there is so incalculably much on earth. For the devil is not only a liar but a murderer as well, he incessantly seeks our life and vents his anger by causing accidents and injury to our bodies. He crushes some and drives others to insanity; some he drowns in water, and many he hounds to suicide or other dreadful catastrophes. Therefore, there is nothing for us to do on earth but to pray without ceasing against this archenemy. For if God did not support us, we would not be safe from him for a single hour" (LC III 115–16; K-W, pp. 455–56).

The last petition of the Lord's Prayer forms the basis of Luther's letter to Bernard Wurzelmann in 1535. In responding to an inquiry from Wurzelmann, a pastor who had reason to believe that a parishioner was possessed by the devil, Luther urges a consistent and fervent use of intercessory prayer based on his own pastoral experience: "The first thing you and your congregation ought to do is this: Pray fervently and oppose Satan with your faith, no matter how stubbornly he resists. About ten years ago we had an experience in this neighborhood with a very wicked demon, and we succeeded in subduing him by perseverance and by unceasing prayer and unquestioning faith. The same will happen among you if you continue in Christ's name to despise that derisive and arrogant spirit and do not cease praying. By this means I have restrained many similar spirits in different places, for the prayer of the Church prevails at last. Consequently you should have no doubt, if you pray in truth and with perseverance, that this wicked spirit will be humbled" (Tappert, p. 42).

Satan and his demonic forces were a reality to be reckoned with in the sixteenth century as they are in the present day. Both then and now, however, there are those who become obsessed with these matters. There is always the danger of spiritual fraud. So Luther warns Wurzelmann that he should "carefully investigate whether that woman might be practicing some fraud by means of which you could be made objects of ridicule. In my own experience (apart entirely from what I have read in books) I have encountered such frauds, and afterward I have reproached myself for my simplicity. The evil spirit takes delight (as he did in the beginning with Adam) in using a woman to make a fool of a man—if he cannot make him godless, as he much prefers to do. . . . Therefore, we should not be inattentive and casual with regard to his fabrications and deeds, his realities and apparitions, but should fight against him with faith and prayer. The

One who he crucified lives. And by his own power the Crucified One again triumphed over his crucifier in order that in the former we too may triumph over the later" (Tappert, pp. 42–43).

Ten years later in 1545, Luther gives more explicit instruction to Pastor Severin Schulze for the exorcism of one oppressed by the devil. Luther counsels the pastor how to proceed with the exorcism. Schulze is instructed to come to the oppressed man "with the deacon along with two or three good men. Confident that you, as pastor of the place, are clothed with the authority of the ministerial office, lay your hands upon him and say, 'Peace be with you, dear brother, from God our Father and from our Lord Jesus Christ' " (Tappert, p. 52). The Creed is to be confessed and the Lord's Prayer prayed over the afflicted man "in a loud and clear voice" closing with these words of invocation and blessing: "O God, almighty Father, who hast told us through thy Son, 'Verily, verily, I say unto you, Whatsoever ye shall ask the Father in my name, he will give it to you'; who hast commanded and encouraged us to pray in his name, 'Ask, and ye shall receive', and who in like manner hast said, 'Call upon me in the day of trouble: I will deliver thee, and thou shalt glorify me', we unworthy sinners, relying on these thy words and commands, pray for thy mercy with such faith as we can muster. Graciously deign to free this man from all evil, and put to nought the work that Satan has done in him, to the honor of thy name And strengthening the faith of believers; through the same Jesus Christ, thy Son, our Lord, who liveth and reigneth with thee, world without end. Amen" (Tappert, p. 52).[17] Luther cites Mark 16:18 and says: "Then, when you depart, lay your hands upon the man again and say, 'These signs shall follow them that believe; they shall lay hands on the sick, and they shall recover' " (Tappert, p. 52).

Since he recognized that the hold of Satan is not easily broken, Luther counsels the pastor to be steadfast and persistent in his struggle. The rite is to be repeated three times. Luther says, "Do this three times, once on each of three successive days. Meanwhile let prayers be said from the chancel of the church, publicly, until God hears them" (Tappert, p. 52). The prayers of the congregation are enlisted for the demonically oppressed man, as Luther does not divorce pastoral prayer from the prayer of the whole Church.[18]

17 Luther's prayer is used in the section entitled "Occult Practices and Demonic Affliction" in *LSB: Pastoral Care Companion* (St. Louis; Concordia, 2007), 360.

18 Here also see, Esko Murto, "An Iron Wall on Our Side: Martin Luther's Understanding of Christian Devotional Life against the Devil" in *Theology Is Eminently Practical: Essays in Honor of John T. Pless*, eds. Jacob Corzine and Bryan Wolfmueller (Fort Wayne: Lutheran Legacy Press, 2012), 129–42.

CHAPTER 8

Pastoral Care of the Grieving

In the Midst of Life: Death

Death was an ever-present reality in Luther's world. Having lost two of his own children to premature death—Elizabeth at seven months and Magdalena at age fourteen—Luther was well acquainted with bereavement. His care for those who experienced the death of a child, parent, or spouse is marked with empathy and firm confidence in the promises of Christ's resurrection. In the place of medieval notions of purgatory and the uncertainty that it evoked, Luther substitutes a view of death framed by the conclusion of the Apostles' Creed: belief in the forgiveness of sins, the resurrection of the body, and life everlasting.

Luther grounds the comfort that he gives in the victory of Christ's cross and resurrection. "The resurrection of Christ has become the death of death."[1] Our Lord's victory over death and the grave guarantees the believer's ultimate triumph. This is reflected in Luther's hymns "In the Very Midst of Life" (*LSB* 755) and "Christ Jesus Lay in Death's Strong Bands" (*LSB* 458). While Luther never prepared a revised funeral liturgy, he contends that Christian funerals ought to "honor and praise that joyous article of our faith, namely, the resurrection of dead, and in order to defy Death, that terrible foe who so shamefully and in so many horrible ways goes on to devour us." Therefore "we do not sing any dirges or doleful songs over our dead and at the grave, but comforting hymns of the forgiveness of sins, of rest, sleep, life, and of the resurrection of departed Christians so that our faith may be strengthened and the people moved to true devotion" (AE 53:326). Masses and prayers for the dead were replaced with evangelical proclamation of Christ's victory over death in sermon and song.

Proper Christian burial is a testimony to the hope of the resurrection. The corpse is treated with dignity and respect in view of the fact Christ Jesus has redeemed body and soul with His blood and guaranteed victory over death in His resurrection. In his lectures on Genesis in 1539, Luther cites the

1 Gerhard Sauter, "Luther on the Resurrection," *Lutheran Quarterly* (Summer 2001): 2008.

provisions Abraham made for his own burial: "Besides this example teaches us that the dead should be buried with special honor and respect because of the faith in and hope of the future resurrection. . . . Therefore there is all the more reason for some reverence among Christians, on account of the article of faith concerning the resurrection of the flesh, lest we seem to be deprived of life and buried like horses and mules" (AE 4:205). Four years later in 1543, still lecturing on Genesis, he comments on the burial of Rachel to incite Christians to bury their dead in such a manner as testifies to the resurrection: "The fathers decorated sepulchers magnificently. They did not throw away the dead like bodies of beast, but they set up memorials of them for a perpetual reminder so that they might be testimonies of the future resurrection, which they believed and expected. Therefore funeral ceremonies and the funeral procession are to be retained, and likewise the weeping and the sympathy, not that there should be prayers for the dead, as Lyra wishes, or that we should fear death, but rather that in death itself we should learn to exercise faith as it struggles against the terrors of death and think that we indeed die and are buried in dishonor but that we will rise again in glory" (AE 6:273–74).

Lord Over Life and Death

God is the Lord over both life and death. Luther often uses Job 1:21 to remind people that God both gives and takes away. Faith is tutored to bless God for both of these divine activities. So Veit Dietrich records words of consolation that Luther spoke to Benedict Pauli, a Wittenberg lawyer whose son had been killed in an accident in 1533. Luther reminds him of biblical figures who grieved over the death of their sons and urges moderation in mourning so as to leave space for consolation, reminding Pauli that we experience more good than evil from God. Luther answers Pauli's fear that God took his son in wrath: "It is enough for us to know that we have a gracious God. Why he permits this or that evil to befall us should not trouble us at all" (Tappert, p. 69).[2]

An example of the evangelical turn in Luther's care for the grieving can be seen in his September 1, 1524, letter to Austrian nobleman Bartholomew von Staremberg, occasioned by the death of his wife, Magdalene. Using Job 1:21, Luther urges Bartholomew to "sing the same song to a dear and faithful God who gave you a dear and faithful wife and has now taken

2 Also note Luther's words in the Genesis lectures: "But who can supply the reason for the things that he sees the Divine Majesty has permitted to happen? Why do we not rather learn with Job that God cannot be called to account and cannot be compelled to give us the reason for everything He does or permits to happen?" (AE 1:144).

her away" (Tappert, pp. 53–54). Luther notes that before this woman was Bartholomew's wife, she was God's own possession. When God takes a person in death, He is simply recalling what is His own. Luther urges Bartholomew to leave off the masses and prayers for the dead. "It is enough," Luther says, "to pray once or twice for her" (Tappert, p. 54). Faith takes God at His Word and does not act in unbelief. Not only are masses for the dead useless, they are unchristian. They serve neither the living nor the dead. Luther concludes with a final blessing that serves to reintegrate Bartholomew to life in the world without his wife: "Christ enlighten and strengthen you in true faith and in love of your neighbor" (Tappert, p. 55).

Queen Mary of Hungary received a letter from Luther dated November 1, 1526. Luther sought to comfort Mary after her husband, King Lewis, was killed in battle. Luther notes that the purpose of this letter is to fulfill Romans 15:4, that is, to use Holy Scripture for patience and comfort so that hope might abound. The letter is actually a dedicatory epistle prefaced to Luther's treatment of four psalms. In speaking to this widow's loss, Luther reminds her that God has provided her with a true bridegroom in Christ: "God has at this time visited you, not in anger or displeasure (as we have every reason to hope) but as a trial and chastisement in order that you may learn to trust in the true Father who is in heaven and be comforted by the true bridegroom, Jesus Christ, who is our brother, and indeed, our very flesh and blood, and in order that Your Majesty may find joy with your true friends and faithful companions, the dear angels, who ever surround and care for us" (Tappert, pp. 57–58). Luther concludes this letter with a reflection on the place of the cross in the life of the Christian, noting that our own smaller crosses are more painful for us than Christ's cross. This is so, he says, "Because we are not so patient as God is, and consequently a smaller cross is more painful to us than Christ's cross" (Tappert, p. 58).

Death may challenge trust in God. Writing to a childhood friend John Reineck after the death of his wife in 1536, Luther addresses the way that death tests our faith in God's good will and His favor toward us: "God has so ordered and limited our life here that we may learn and exercise the knowledge of his very good will so that we may test and discover whether we love and esteem his will more than ourselves and everything that he has given us to have and love on earth. And although the inscrutable goodness of the divine will is hidden (as is God himself) from the old Adam as something so great and profound that man finds no pleasure in it, but only grief and lamentation, we nevertheless have his holy and sure Word which reveals to us this hidden will of his and gladdens the heart of the believer.

For it is written everywhere in the Scriptures that when he chastises his children, he does so out of pure grace and not wrath" (Tappert, p. 69). In the face of such chastisement, Luther counsels Reineck to take refuge in God's gracious promise: "If we are sure of God's grace, everything will be well with us, even if, like Job we lose all that we have" (Tappert, p. 70). Finally, Luther reminds Reineck that his wife departed this vale of tears in a Christian way. In this way, her death is an example to us that ought to ready us so that "we too may leave our sinful carcasses in like fashion and proceed from this wretchedness to our home and fatherland" (Tappert, p. 70).

Grief within Faith

Luther's letter of January 10, 1539, to John von Taubenheim, whose wife had died, expresses this same theme. Recognizing that the unruly flesh fights against God's good will and too readily gives way to unbelief and despair, Luther urges the widower to rest in God's peace: "In the struggle with your grief let the peace of God, which passes all understanding, keep the victory, even if the flesh gags and grumbles. I am aware that, instructed by God's Word without my counsel, you yourself know that the peace of God is not a matter of the five senses or of the understanding but goes beyond these and is a matter of faith" (Tappert, p. 71).

Yet Luther does not suggest a stoic approach to grief. He deals with those who mourn with empathy and compassion but without allowing them to wallow in their loss. Using 1 Thessalonians 4:13, Luther urges the bereaved to moderation in their sorrow. To grieve is understandable, as God has made human beings creatures of flesh and blood complete with emotions. So, in a letter to Catherine Metzler after her son had died in 1538 while a student at Wittenberg, Luther consoles the boy's mother, saying: "It is natural and right that you should grieve, especially for one who is of your own flesh and blood. For God has not created us to be without feeling or to be like stones and sticks, but it is his will that we mourn and bewail our dead. Otherwise it would appear that we had no love, particularly in the case of members of our own family" (Tappert, p. 72).

In similar way Luther addresses Ambrose Berndt, a former student whose wife, Margaret, and infant son, John, died in childbirth in early 1532. Luther observes that it would be inhuman not to be distressed by such a tragic death: "For the great and godly affection which binds a husband to his wife is so strong that it cannot easily be shaken off, and this feeling of sorrow is not displeasing to God, if only it be held in check, since it is an expression of what God has firmly implanted in you. Nor would I account you a man, to say nothing of a good husband, if you could throw off your grief" (Tappert, p. 62). However, the mourning is to be constrained within the boundaries of faith and hope. Luther continues: "Nevertheless, my dear Ambrose, I allow your mourning only in so far as it is not contrary to the will of God. For it is necessary to put a limit on sorrow and grief" (Tappert, p. 62). Then Luther proceeds to counsel Ambrose to ponder and reflect on the gift he was given in his Christian wife. The loss of such a human treasure surely evokes painful sorrow.

In and through the understandable sorrow, Luther calls on Ambrose to rejoice that while a physical gift was withdrawn by God, a spiritual gift was given. Luther identifies the spiritual gift as a Christian death died in faith while Margaret was fulfilling her vocation as wife and mother: "On the other hand, you must also reflect on the fact that this very death of your wife ought to make you exceedingly happy before God inasmuch as she died in childbirth, that is, in the performance of her God-given duty and in the exercise of her proper calling. Moreover, she did this with a resolute spirit and firm faith in Christ. Knowing that she was facing death, she confessed him again and again, called upon Christ alone, and offering herself wholly to God, was resigned to his will. In addition, it is to be reckoned a singular blessing that she was graciously enabled by God, amid her great suffering, to bear you a son, John, who was baptized and then buried together with his mother" (Tappert, p. 63).

In comforting the grieving, Luther holds together the creational aspects of human life with the gift of faith in Christ bestowed through the Gospel. The significance of a child or spouse is recognized and affirmed, but these gifts are held within the context of God's grace in Christ Jesus that embraces all of life. This is further seen in Luther's letter to Thomas Zink, the father of Johannes, a young man who died in April 1532 while a student at Wittenberg. Luther writes tenderly of Johannes's life recounting that he was a pious and well-behaved student. Once again Luther recognizes that the grief of parents is not sub-Christian or abnormal: "It is only natural that your son's death and the report of it should distress and grieve you and your dear wife, his parents. I do not blame you for this, for all of us, and I in particular, are stricken with sorrow. Yet I admonish you that you should much rather thank God for giving you such a good, pious son and for deeming you worthy of all the pains and money you have so well invested in him. But let this be your best comfort, as it is ours that he fell asleep (rather than departed) decently and softly with such a fine testimony of his faith on his lips that we all marveled. There can be as little doubt that he is with God, his true Father, in eternal blessedness, as there can be doubt that the Christian faith is true. Such a beautiful Christian end as his cannot fail to lead heavenward" (Tappert, p. 65). So Luther urges these bereaved parents to give thanks for their son for "now he is in a place which he would not exchange for all the world, even for a moment" (Tappert, p. 65). Once again echoing the Pauline admonition to grieve but not as the pagans do without hope (see 1 Thessalonians 4:13), Luther continues: "Grieve in such a way, therefore, as to console yourselves. For you have not lost him, but have sent him on ahead of you to be kept in everlasting blessedness. Saint Paul says that we should not mourn over the departed, over those who have fallen, asleep, like the heathen" (Tappert, p. 65).

Cheating Death

Hope lives in the certainty that those who die in the faith are secure with the Lord. This theme is prominent in Luther's correspondence with those who are grieving. Luther writes to his close friend and fellow pastor Conrad Cordatus, whose infant son died in 1530. He reminds Cordatus that before the child was his son, he was and is God's own son, assuring him that his child is "safer there than here" (Tappert, p. 60). For now he is beyond the grasp of sin and the devil. In a similar fashion, Luther consoles a Mr. and Mrs. Matthias Knudsen whose son, a Wittenberg student, died in 1531. He says their son had cheated death by dying in saving faith: "Your son has cheated the world and the devil while we are still in danger of being overcome by them and are exposed to all the perils against which he is now secure" (Tappert, p. 62). Death brings the Christian's Baptism to its divinely appointed consummation since, through physical death, the believer is delivered from the daily dying that marks the life of repentance and faith.

What about Suicide?

Luther's evangelical approach is especially evident in the pastoral care he provided for those who mourn a death by suicide. Luther did not believe that all suicides were necessarily damned. In addressing the widow of a man who committed suicide, Luther writes, "That your husband inflicted injury upon himself may be explained by the devil's power over our members. He may have directed your husband's hand, even against his own free will. For if your husband had done what he did of his own free will, he would surely not have come to himself and turned to Christ with such a confession of faith. How often the devil breaks arms, legs, backs, and all our members! He can be the master of the body and its members against our will" (Tappert, p. 59). Luther's letter reflects his understanding of the devil's power.

When we pray the last petition of the Lord's Prayer, we petition the Lord to deliver us from self-slaughter. In his treatment of "Deliver us from evil" in the Large Catechism, Luther says, "Nevertheless, this petition includes all the evil that may befall us under the devil's kingdom: poverty, disgrace, death, and, in short, all the tragic misery and heartache, of which there is so incalculably much on earth. For because the devil is not only a liar but a murderer as well, he incessantly seeks our life by causing accidents and injury to our bodies. *He crushes some and drives others to insanity; some he drowns in water, and many he hounds to suicide or other dreadful catastrophes.* Therefore, there is nothing for us to do on earth but to pray without ceasing against this archenemy. For if God did not support us, we would not be safe from him for a single hour" (LC III 114–16; K-W, pp. 455–56, emphasis added). In a Table Talk of 1532, Luther says, "I don't share the opinion that suicides are certainly to be damned. My reason is that they do not wish to kill themselves but are overcome by the power of the devil. They are like a man who is murdered in the woods by a robber. However, this ought not be taught to the common people, lest Satan be given the opportunity to cause slaughter, and I recommend that the popular custom be strictly adhered to according to which (the suicide's corpse) is not carried over the threshold, etc. Such a person does not die by free choice or by law, but our Lord God will dispatch them as he executes a person through a robber. Magistrates should treat them quite strictly, although it is not plain that their souls are damned. However, they are examples by which our Lord God wishes to show that the devil is powerful and also that we should be diligent in prayer. But for these examples, we would not fear God. Hence he must teach this way" (AE 54:29). Martin Brecht points to another instance to confirm the consistency of Luther's pastoral approach: "When a pastor was troubled in conscience for having performed a church funeral for a suicide, contrary to the usual custom, Luther consoled him. It had not really been the suicide victim himself who had done this deed, but the devil. The victim was therefore not responsible for his action. Nevertheless, in order to warn others against doing so, Luther insisted that attempted suicide should be punished."[3]

---

3 Brecht, *Martin Luther: The Preservation of the Church 1532–1546* (Minneapolis: Fortress Press, 1993), 283–84.

Without minimizing the sinful nature of suicide, Luther handles these cases with merciful tenderness, recognizing the nature of Satan as a murderer and liar from the beginning who temporarily overcomes even the baptized believer casting him or her into the darkness of despair, even to the point of self-murder. Yet suicide is not a sin too large for the Lamb of God, who takes away the sin of the whole world. Pastorally, Luther directs those who grieve over the suicide of a loved one to the wounds of Christ and away from self-tormenting worries about the eternal fate of the deceased.

Luther's Funeral Preaching

Examples of Luther's funeral preaching can be found in the two sermons he delivered on the occasion of the death of Duke John (1468–1532), Elector of Saxony. Duke John died on August 16, 1532; Luther preached his first sermon on Sunday morning, August 18. Luther preached a second sermon the following Thursday, August 22. Both were delivered at the Castle Church.

In the first sermon, based on 1 Thessalonians 4:13–14, Luther seeks to console the congregation through preaching. In this sermon, we see Luther making a move that he often does in addressing the bereaved. He affirms that their grief is altogether natural. There is no virtue in trying to eliminate the reality of sorrow by attempting to fabricate a stoic strength in the face of death. The Scriptures, in fact, give us permission to mourn our dead. Paul does not disapprove of grief in his letter to the Thessalonians. So Luther says, "For the steadfast man is not the one who thinks himself so strong that he refuses to be touched when a good friend has slipped away; rather the Christian is one who is hurt but yet endures it in such a way that the spirit rules the flesh. For God has not created man to be a stick or a stone. He has given him five senses and a heart of flesh in order that he may love his friends, be angry with his enemies, and to lament and grieve when his dear friends suffer evil" (AE 51:232–33). Since our Lord Jesus Christ wept at the grave of his friend Lazarus, we are to be done with "this unprofitable chatter which would make sticks and stones of us and forbid us to weep and sorrow over the deceased" (AE 51:233). This discourse on the appropriateness of grief serves as a preface to Luther's sermon; he really aims to proclaim the death and resurrection of Christ for the consolation of his hearers.

Into the bitterness of our grief, God has mixed "good sugar," says Luther (AE 51:233). That is, the sweetness of the Gospel, "'that Jesus died and rose again' [I Thess. 4:14]" and makes "it also certain that God will bring with him those who died in Christ and will not let them simply remain where we think they remain, but will bring them to himself" (AE 51:233). With the simple line from 1 Thessalonians 4:14 as the anchor for the sermon, Luther goes on to urge the worshipers to hold the death of the Elector and their own deaths under the death of Christ. The death of Christ, Luther contends, has a bitterness that is lacking in our death, for His death is for our sin, and therefore it is much more horrible than any other death. We are to learn to "mingle" and "cover" our dying with the death of Christ. No higher consolation can be found than to contemplate the death of Christ and "to see how mighty and glorious it has become and how it has devoured all other deaths, so that by comparison, this death is the most grievous and cruel of all" (AE 51:234–35).

Rightly contemplating Christ's death means that we are enabled not to see merely the corpse of the Elector but that of Christ Jesus: "Beloved, look not at this dead body; you have something higher and better to contemplate, namely, the death and resurrection of Jesus Christ. If you gaze steadfastly at this mirror and image, at Christ the Lord, who died and rose again, you will see where you will go and where those will go who have not fallen asleep in Christ, namely, that God intends to bring with him you and all others who have been baptized and have fallen asleep in Christ, because he has wrapped them in Christ's death and included them in his resurrection and does not intend to leave them lying under the ground, even though for our reason and five senses there is no reason why this should be so, in order that faith may find room and we learn to trust God even in that which we do not see" (AE 51:235). We are to see our death through the lens of Christ's death and in this way comprehend the mystery that these corruptible and perishable bodies "sown in dishonor," to use Paul's words, will be raised in honor with Christ.

Only after speaking of Christ does the preacher turn to the deceased himself. Luther masterfully balances his language about the departed. "I shall not praise him now for his great virtues, but rather let him remain a sinner like all the rest of us, who also purpose to go to the judgment and hand over to our Lord God many a grievous sin, as we too hold steadfast to that article which is called 'the forgiveness of sins' " (AE 51:236). Therefore Luther says that it would be pointless to "make out that our beloved lord was altogether pure" (AE 51:236). The Elector was a sinner for whom Christ died. That is the bedrock of Christian confidence.

Yet this forgiven sinner also had a vocation: he was a Christian prince. Luther is not ashamed to extol the Elector's faithfulness. Just two years before, at the Diet of Augsburg, the Elector suffered a "real death" (AE

51:237), says Luther, in that he openly confessed Christ, risking everything for the sake of the Gospel. This was the Elector's real "manly death" in contrast to the "child's death" that marked the end of his earthly life. The Elector had already endured the real death of scorn and contempt at Augsburg; his earthly passing Luther describes as a "baby death" (AE 51:238), for the Elector was taken by the Lord into the heavenly kingdom without fear or trembling. Luther repeats the imagery of the Elector being wrapped up and concealed in the death of Christ.

Then Luther goes on to describe the beauty beyond telling that will bedeck the body of the Elector when Christ, who has devoured death, returns in glory. Using the death of Duke John as an example of a Christian way of dying, Luther returns to the potency of Christ's death for us and exhorts the congregation to forsake their own self-made forms of holiness and cling to the divine promises alone that we have in "his dear baptism, his gospel, his Word and sacraments" (AE 51:242).

APPENDIX

Baptism as Means of Consolation in Luther's Pastoral Theology

This essay was originally given at the International Congress for Luther Research meeting in Copenhagen in August 2002. It was published in *Concordia Theological Quarterly* (January 2003): 19–32.

"Ah, dear Christians, let us not value or treat this unspeakable gift so half-heartedly. For baptism is our only comfort and the doorway to all of God's possessions and to the communion of all the saints. To this end may God help us," writes Luther in his baptismal booklet appended to the second edition of the Small Catechism in 1529 (K-W, p. 373). By including his *Taufbüchlein* of 1526 in the catechism, Luther accented not only the liturgical significance of Baptism but also the value of this Sacrament for the Christian life. Luther identifies Baptism as the believer's "only comfort." It is this theme that will be examined in representative pastoral pieces in Luther's writings after the publication of the catechisms. The language of the catechisms on Baptism shaped Luther's use of Baptism for the consolation of Christians.[1]

While Baptism was featured quite prominently in the Early Church, its place was diminished in the Middle Ages. There was little catechetical literature to tutor the faithful on the significance of Baptism. In fact, the chief feature of Baptism seemed to be that of initiation. Baptism was the beginning point on the sacramental continuum, but it had little significance for the ongoing spiritual life as the Eucharist, and especially penance, overshadowed Baptism. By way of contrast Luther did not limit Baptism to the moment of the rite but asserted the enduring benefits of Baptism

1 See Albrecht Peters, *Kommentar zu Luthers Katechismen Band 4: Die Taufe. Das Abendmahl* (Goettingen: Vandenhoeck & Ruprecht, 1993), 71–126 for a treatment of Luther's theology of Baptism in the catechisms. Also see Klaus Schwarzwäller, *Fuelle Des Lebens Luthers Kleiner Katechismus* (Muenster: Lit Verlag, 1998), 219–43.

both for daily life and finally for the approach of death itself.[2] For Luther, Baptism is no mere rite of initiation on the spectrum of sacramental acts, but the basis and content of the Christian's life that is brought to completion only in the resurrection of the body.

In May 1531, Luther received word that his mother was seriously ill in Mansfeld. The sickness would prove to be fatal, as Margaret would die the next month, June 30, just a little over a year after the death of her husband. On May 20, Luther writes a tender letter to his mother, alluding especially to John 16:33 ("I have said these things to you, that in me you may have peace. In the world you will have tribulation. But take heart; I have overcome the world"). In this letter, Luther rejoices that his mother is well instructed in God's fatherly goodness and grace and urges her to accept this suffering as a slight affliction in comparison with the sufferings of Christ. Luther writes, "You know the real basis and foundation of your salvation, on which you must rest your confidence in this and all troubles, namely Jesus Christ, the cornerstone, who will never waver or fail us, nor allow us to sink and perish, for he is the Saviour and he is called the Saviour of all poor sinners, of all who face tribulation and death, of all who rely on him and call on his name" (Tappert, p. 34).[3] Throughout the letter, Luther points to Christ's passion and resurrection as the source of confidence in the face of death. Luther's imagery for the threat of death is vivid: "You can show your teeth, but you cannot bite. For God has given us the victory through Christ Jesus our Lord, to whom be praise and thanks. Amen" (Tappert, p. 35). Christ is not the accuser and judge but Savior and Comforter.

But where is such a Christ to be found? Luther directs his mother to Word and Sacrament. Near the end of the letter Luther writes, "To such knowledge, I say, God has graciously called you. In the gospel, in Baptism, and in the Sacrament (of the Altar) you possess his sign and seal of this vocation, and as long as you hear him addressing you in these, you will have no trouble or danger. Be of good cheer, then, and thank him joyfully for such great grace, for he who has begun a good work in you will perform until the day of Jesus Christ. We cannot help ourselves in such matters.

2 See Mark Tranvik, "Luther on Baptism," *Lutheran Quarterly* (Spring 1999): 75–90 for an overview of Luther's baptismal teaching. Other helpful studies include Lorenz Groenvik, *Der Taufe in der Theologie Martin Luther* (Abo: Abo Akademi, 1968); Robert Kolb, "What Benefit Does the Soul Receive from a Handful of Water?: Luther's Preaching on Baptism, 1528–1539," *Concordia Journal* (October 1999): 346–63; David Lotz, "The Sacrament of Salvation: Luther on Baptism and Justification," *Trinity Seminary Review* (September 1984): 3–13; and Jonathan Trigg, *Baptism in the Theology of Martin Luther* (Leiden: Brill, 1994).

3 For a very thorough treatment of Luther's use of letters as tools for pastoral care, see Gerhard Ebeling, *Luthers Seelsorge an seinen Briefen dargestellt* (Tuebigen: J. C. B. Mohr, 1997), though Ebeling overlooks the significance of Baptism in these letters.

We can accomplish nothing against sin, death, and the devil by our own works" (Tappert, pp. 35–36).

While Luther only mentions Baptism in this letter, it is significant that Luther directs his mother to Baptism, along with the Gospel and the Lord's Supper, as the place where God speaks. For Luther, pastoral care does not direct the dying Christian to her own thoughts or deeds but to the promises of God given in the *externum verbum* of Gospel, Baptism, and Supper.[4] Earlier in this letter, Luther reminded his mother that God had brought her to the knowledge of salvation and "not allowed her to remain in papal error, by which we were taught to rely on our own works and the holiness of monks and to consider this only comfort of ours, our Saviour, not as a comforter but as a severe judge and tyrant, so that we could only flee from him to Mary and the saints and not expect of him any grace or comfort" (Tappert, p. 35). Luther sets this approach in contrast to Christ, who reconciles sinners to the Father rather than visiting them with wrath and condemnation.

In his 1519 treatise *The Holy and Blessed Sacrament of Baptism,* Luther complained that the papists ignored Baptism in favor of self-made satisfactions: "They go so far as to disregard their baptism, as if they had no more need of it beyond the fact of having once been baptized. They do not know that baptism is in force all through life, even until death, yes—as said above—even to the Last Day. For this reason they presume to find some other way of blotting out sin, namely by works. So for themselves and all others, they create evil, terrified, and uncertain consciences, and despair at the hour of death. They do not know how they stand with God, thinking that by sin they have lost their baptism and that it profits them no more" (AE 35:37). Now in this letter to his dying mother, Luther emphasizes the efficacy of Baptism throughout this life until it is brought to consummation in the resurrection of the flesh.

On June 29, 1534, Luther writes to John Ruehel, chancellor to Count Albert of Mansfeld and a relative of Luther by marriage. Luther had learned of Ruehel's illness and his impatience in suffering. After comforting Ruehel with the words of 2 Corinthians 12:9 ("My strength is made perfect in weakness"), Luther writes, "The realization that you have been called by this Man, that you have been blessed by a knowledge, desire, and love for his Word, and that you have been sealed therein by his Baptism and Sacrament should surely make you more cheerful. What more do you expect of Him who has inwardly given you such love toward him and has outwardly given

4 On this *extra nos* accent, note Luther's defense in his 1527 lectures on Titus: "If we were able to enter heaven without outward things, there would be no necessity to send Christ" (AE 29:83).

you such seals and such a testimony of his grace? Dear doctor, behold the good things you possess at his hands rather than what you suffer. The balance is tipped immeasurably in favor of the former" (Tappert, pp. 37–38). Luther draws Ruehel away from what he suffers to the fact that Christ has called him to faith. The gifts of Christ outweigh all pain and grief.

After reminding Ruehel that God is able to restore him to health, Luther quotes the apostle Paul: "Whether we live or die, we are the Lord's" (Romans 14:8). Luther comments, "Yes, indeed, *Domini* in the genitive and in the nominative—in the genitive (we are the Lord's) because we are his dwelling place, his members, and in the nominative (we are lords) because we rule over all things through faith, which is our victory, and because, thanks be to God, we trample the lion and the dragon underfoot" (Tappert, p. 38). While Luther does not explicitly connect Romans 14 to Baptism, it seems to be implicit in the comfort that he gives to Ruehel for it is in Baptism that God claims sinners as His own children. Hence this letter of comfort echoes Luther's words from *The Holy and Blessed Sacrament of Baptism*: "This blessed sacrament of baptism helps you because God allies himself with you and becomes one with you in a gracious covenant of comfort" (AE 35:33). Through faith, which alone can apprehend the blessings of Baptism, the believer is a lord over death and the devil. Recall the words of the Large Catechism: "In baptism, therefore, every Christian has enough to study and practice all his or her life. Christians always have enough to do to firmly believe what baptism promises and brings—victory over death and the devil, the forgiveness of sin, God's grace, the entire Christ, and the Holy Spirit with his gifts" (LC IV 41–42; K-W, p. 461).

In a Table Talk from autumn 1532 recorded by Conrad Cordatus, Luther addresses predestination from the perspective of Baptism. Cordatus reports that Luther warned against speculation regarding election saying that "when a man begins to dispute about it, it is like a fire that cannot be extinguished, and the more he disputes the more he despairs" (Tappert, p. 122; WA TR No. 263).[5] God shows Himself to be opposed to these troublesome and terrifying thoughts. It is for this reason, says Luther,

5 Also see the Table Talk recorded by Caspar Heydenreich on February 18, 1542, where Luther addresses predestination (Tappert, p. 131–38; WA TR No5658a). Here Luther counsels those who are troubled by questions of divine election not to attempt to "climb into heaven" but to "begin at the bottom with the incarnate Son and with your terrible original sin" (Tappert, p. 133). Luther says "God did not come down from heaven to make you uncertain about predestination or cause you to despise the Sacraments. He instituted them to make you more certain and to drive such speculations out of your mind" (Tappert, p. 133). Luther continues: "These speculations about predestination are of the devil. If they assault you, say: 'I am a son of God. I have been baptized. I believe in Jesus Christ, who was crucified for me. Let me alone, devil' " (Tappert, p. 134).

that God "instituted Baptism, the Word, and the Sacrament as signs to counteract it" (Tappert, p. 122).

Luther sees Baptism along with the preaching of the Gospel and the Sacrament of the Altar as the only sure defense and shield against the despair incited by predestination. Luther says "We should rely on these and say: 'I have been baptized. I believe in Jesus Christ. I have received the Sacrament. What do I care if I have been predestined or not?' In Christ, God has furnished us with a foundation on which to stand and from which we can go up to heaven. He is the only way and the only gate that leads to the Father. If we despise this foundation and in the devil's name start building at the roof, we shall surely fall. If only we are able to believe that the promises have been spoken by God and see behind them the one who has spoken them, we shall magnify that Word. But because we hear it as it comes to us through the lips of a man, we are apt to pay as little attention to it as to the mooing of a cow" (Tappert, p. 122.; WA TR, No. 2631b).

From this Table Talk we may observe several aspects of Luther's understanding of Baptism. First, Baptism is a sign of God's favor in Christ and is based on His promises. In *The Babylonian Captivity of the Church*, Luther writes, "Now the first thing to be considered about baptism is the divine promise. . . . The promise must be set far above all the glitter of works, vows, religious orders and whatever else man has introduced, for on it all our salvation depends" (AE 36:58–59). While in 1519 Luther does speak of Baptism as a sign and token that separates Christians from the unbaptized, Baptism is not merely an identifying mark or badge. The sign is fulfilled in what it signifies, namely dying and rising in Christ. Therefore Luther writes, "The significance of baptism—the dying or drowning of sin—is not fulfilled completely in this life. Indeed this does not happen until man passes through bodily death and completely decays to dust. As we can plainly see, the sacrament or sign of baptism is quickly over. But the spiritual baptism, the drowning of sin, which it signifies, lasts as long as we live and is completed only in death. Then it is that a person is completely sunk in baptism, and that which baptism signifies comes to pass" (AE 35:30). A similar point is made in the following year in *The Babylonian Captivity of the Church*: "Baptism, then, signifies two things—death and resurrection, that is full and complete justification. When the minister immerses the child in the water it signifies death, and when he draws it forth, again it signifies life. Thus Paul expounds it in Rom. 6(:4): 'We were buried therefore with Christ by baptism into death, so that as Christ was raised from the dead by the glory of the Father, we too might walk in the newness of life.' This death and resurrection we call the new creation, regeneration, and spiritual birth. This should not be understood only allegorically as the death of sin and the life of grace, as many understand it, but as actual death and resurrection. For baptism is not a false sign" (AE 36:68).

Baptism is an efficacious sign because of God's word of promise. "Now, the first thing to be considered about baptism is the divine promise," says Luther (AE 36:58). Faith clings to the promise: "For just as the truth of the divine promise, once pronounced over us, continues until death, so our faith in it ought never to cease, but be nourished and strengthened until death by the continual remembrance of this promise made to us in baptism" (AE 36:59).

Second, Baptism can be trusted because it is the work of the triune God. In *The Babylonian Captivity of the Church*, Luther asserts: "For man baptizes, and yet he does not baptize. He baptizes in that he performs the work of immersing the person to be baptized; he does not baptize, because in doing so he acts not on his own authority but in God's stead. Hence, we ought to receive baptism at human hands just as if Christ himself, indeed God, himself, were baptizing us with his own hands" (AE 36:62). This same point is made again in the Large Catechism: "To be baptized in God's name is to be baptized not by human beings but by God himself. Although it is performed by human hands, it is nevertheless truly God's own act. From this fact everyone can easily conclude that it is of much greater value than the work of any human being or saint. For what human work can possibly be greater than God's work?" (LC IV 10; K-W, pp. 457–58).

Therefore, Luther urges those who are troubled by satanic assaults on faith to rely on Baptism. Baptism is to be used as weaponry against Satan as he attacks the conscience: "Thus, we must regard baptism and put it to use in such a way that we may draw strength and comfort from it when our sins or conscience oppress us, and say: 'But I am baptized! And if I have been baptized, I have the promise that I shall be saved and have eternal life, both in body and soul' " (LC IV 44–45; K-W, p. 462). And again, "Thus we see what a great and excellent thing baptism is, which snatches us from the jaws of the devil and makes us God's own, overcomes and takes away sin and daily strengthens the new person, and always endures and remains until we pass out of this misery into eternal glory" (LC IV 83; K-W, p. 466).

Baptism also consoles those who mourn. Caspar Heydenreich, a frequent guest in Luther's home and court chaplain to the Duchess Catherine of Saxony, was away from home when his wife gave birth to a son who died soon after birth. On April 24, 1545, Luther writes Heydenreich a brief note of sympathy. Luther does not fail to recognize the distress that his friend undergoes on account of his absence at the birth and death of his son. Yet, Luther urges Heydenreich to take comfort in the knowledge that his son was baptized. "Lay aside your sorrowing. Rejoice, rather, because he was reborn in Christ and because you will see him in glory whom you have not seen in this wretched world" (Tappert, p. 80; WA Br XI 76).

Luther treasures Baptism as a means of comfort because Baptism delivers the benefits on Jesus' cross. This can be seen in a sermon that Luther preached on the occasion of the Baptism of Bernhard, son of Prince John of Anhalt on April 2, 1540. Using the Baptism of Jesus in Matthew 3:13–17 as his text, Luther sees Baptism as the location of a "beautiful, glorious exchange" where Christ takes upon Himself the sin and guilt of the sinner and bestows on the sinner His righteousness and holiness: "Is not this a beautiful, glorious exchange, by which Christ, who is wholly innocent and holy, not only takes upon himself another's sin, that is my sin and guilt, but also clothes and adorns me, who am nothing but sin, with his own innocence and purity? And then besides dies the shameful death of the Cross for the sake of my sins, through which I have deserved death and condemnation, and grants me his righteousness, in order that I may live with him eternally in glorious and unspeakable joy. Through this blessed exchange, in which Christ changes places with us (something the heart can only grasp in faith), and through nothing else, are we freed from sin and death and given his righteousness and life as our own" (AE 51:316).[6]

Faith receives all that Christ has done on the cross in Baptism. In the Large Catechism, Luther comments that both cross and Baptism are gifts to be received and not works to be done. "Thus you see plainly that baptism is not a work that we do but that it is a treasure that God gives us and faith grasps, just as the Lord Christ upon the cross is not a work but a treasure placed in the setting of the Word and offered to us in the Word and received by faith" (LC IV 37; K-W, p. 461). In language reminiscent of the Large

6 Tranvik observes: "Following Paul in Romans 6:4, Luther sees baptism as the way the cross and resurrection become contemporaneous with the believer. Baptism effects the 'joyous exchange' (*froehliche Wechsel*), a term Luther used frequently to express his understanding of the atonement" ("Luther on Baptism," 79). Also see Robert Kolb: "One of the Pauline themes regarding baptism which Luther employed from his earliest treatments of the sacrament, that of dying and rising with Christ (Romans 6:3–11; Col. 2:11–15), is used in this commentary (Galatians 1535) in connection with his presentation of the justification of the sinner before God. It occurs particularly in the context of Luther's image of the 'joyous exchange' of the sinner's unrighteousness for Christ's righteousness. Thus, even in the absence of many explicit references to baptism, in this most important work of Luther's appears one more confirmation of the thesis that Luther's doctrine of justification through faith was shaped, at least in part, by the baptismal theology of the apostle, as expressed above all in Romans 6:3–11 and Colossians 2:11–15." Robert Kolb, "God Kills to Make Alive: Romans 6 and Luther's Understanding of Justification (1535)," *Lutheran Quarterly* (Spring 1998): 34.

Catechism, Luther preaches, "Such knowledge and faith produces a joyful heart, which is certain and can say: I know of no more sins, for they are all lying on Christ's back. Now, they can never lie both upon him and upon us. Therefore no one can say that he makes satisfaction for sin through his own righteousness or discipline, for atonement and redemption of sin belongs to Christ alone. But Christ is neither my work nor yours nor any man's work. Nor are they his body and blood, which he sacrificed for our sins; he is true God, true man, who bears the sins of the whole world. But he takes them and drowns and smothers them in baptism and the Cross, and lets you proclaim that he has given his body for you and poured out his blood for the forgiveness of your sins" (AE 51:317).

Baptism, therefore, gives the stricken conscience the consolation of God's favor because it is God's work. Again in words that echo the Large Catechism, Luther draws on the Baptism of Jesus as the template for the Christian's Baptism when he proclaims that "baptism is not a useless, empty thing, as the sectarians blasphemously say, but in it all righteousness is fulfilled" (AE 51:318). In Baptism, sins are forgiven, and faith is fortified. Luther continues: "Hence, not only are sins forgiven in baptism, but we are also made sure and certain that God is well pleased with it that he together with Christ and his Holy Spirit, propose to be present when it is administered and he himself will be the baptizer; although this glorious revelation of the divine majesty does not now occur visibly, as it did that time on the Jordan, since it is sufficient that it occurred once as a witness and a sign" (AE 51:318–19).

Luther sees the Baptism of Jesus as a manifestation of the Gospel. We are to look on the Lord's Baptism in the Jordan with eyes of faith and so Luther says, "Interpret this glorious revelation and divine radiance and splendor which shone forth above the baptism of Christ as happening for us" (AE 51:319).[7]

Engaging in a catechetical polemic against those who would make of Baptism only a sign like a brand that marks a sheep, Luther argues that

---

7 The year after Luther preached this sermon, he wrote his catechism hymn, "To Jordan Came the Christ, Our Lord" (see *LSB* 406, 407). Using the Baptism of Jesus in the Jordan as a basis for this hymn, Luther sets in hymnic form many of the themes in the 1540 sermon, especially the linkage between Christ's atonement and Baptism. See Robin Leaver, "Luther's Catechism Hymns: 5. Baptism" *Lutheran Quarterly* (Summer 1998): 161–69. Leaver notes the parallelism between the Small Catechism's treatment of Baptism and the stanzas of this hymn. Note also how the hymn accents the comfort that faith is given through the Word and promise of the triune God in Baptism as Baptism is a bath that washes away transgression and quenches the bitterness of death (stanza 1), bestows the Spirit in the water (stanza 2), causes the Trinity to dwell with us (stanza 4), gives the blessing of salvation and makes one a joyful heir of heaven (stanza 5), and brings healing and pardon, freeing us from sins inherited from Adam and committed by ourselves (stanza 7).

because God's Word has been added to the water, the Word creates and effects what it proclaims. "For where the Word of God, by which he created heaven and earth and all things, is present, there God himself is present with his power and might" (AE 51:320). The Holy Trinity acts in Baptism. "For when it is done in his name it is done indeed by the Holy Trinity" (AE 51:321). Luther exhorts the congregation to look not at the hand of the minister who administers Baptism but to the Word of God that establishes Baptism as a bath of regeneration.

Luther then makes a decisive move in the sermon to more firmly link cross and Baptism. This he does by using John 19:34 and 1 John 5:16 to establish the point that to be baptized is to be washed in the blood of Christ.

Luther sees in the mingled blood and water flowing from the side of the crucified Christ an image of Baptism. Likewise Luther maintains that when the apostle refers to Christ as coming not only by water, but with water and blood (1 John 5:6), "he is always wanting to mingle the blood in the baptism in order that we may see in it the innocent, rosy-red blood of Christ. For human eyes, it is true, there appears to be nothing there but pure white water, but St. John wants us to open the inward and spiritual eyes of faith in order to see, not only water, but also the blood of our Lord Jesus Christ" (AE 51:325).[8] So to be baptized is to be washed and renewed by the blood of Christ's atoning death. Baptism is now the place where God has located the blood that brings forgiveness. Luther continues: "This

---

8 Compare with stanza 7 of Luther's baptismal hymn:

"All that the mortal eye beholds
Is water as we pour it.
Before the eye of faith unfolds
The pow'r of Jesus' merit.
For here it sees the crimson flood
To all our ills bring healing;
The wonders of his precious blood
The love of God revealing,
Assuring His own pardon" (*LSB* 406:7).

Quitmeyer's translation fails to fully convey Luther's thought as Luther does not speak generically of Baptism as an assurance or even revelation of God's love but of Baptism as the agency of liberation from the sin of Adam as well as our own through the blood of Christ. Note the original German text:

"Das Aug allein das Wasser siht,
Wie Menschen Wasser giessen;
Der Glaub im Geist die Kraft versteht
Des Bluttes Jesu Christi,
Und ist vor ihm ein rote Flut,
Von Christi Blut gefaerbet,
Die allen Schaden heilen tut,
Von Adam her geerbet,
Auch von uns selbst begangen" (WA 35:468–470).

blood and its merit and power he put into baptism, in order that in baptism we might receive it. For whenever a person receives baptism in faith this is the same as if he were visibly washed and cleansed of sin with the blood of Christ. For we do not attain the forgiveness of sins through our work, but rather through the death and the shedding of the blood of the Son of God. But he takes this forgiveness and tucks it into baptism" (AE 51:325).

Luther concludes the sermon urging his hearers to "magnify and value our precious holy baptism" as a "true image and sign, erected by God himself, in which we surely find and meet with his grace" (AE 51:327–28). The conclusion of the 1540 sermon recalls Luther's praise of Baptism in the Large Catechism: "No greater jewel, therefore, can adorn our body and soul than baptism, for through it we become completely holy and blessed, which no work on earth can acquire" (LC IV 46; K-W, p. 462).

In summary, Luther sees Baptism as an evangelical means of consolation in times of *Anfechtung* as well as physical suffering because it draws the believer outside of himself into Christ's saving death. The fact that Baptism is external provides faith with a reliable anchorage outside of wavering emotions. The certainty of Baptism is to be found in the trustworthiness of God's promise and work. Mark Tranvik aptly describes Luther's position: "Luther also underscored the importance of the external sign because of faith's fragility. He likens faith to 'butter in the sunshine.' While Luther will always maintain that trust in the promise makes baptism efficacious, he is wary of focusing on faith: 'One must believe, but we neither should nor can know it for certain.' Therefore, one dare not base his baptism on his faith. For who can be sure if he really believes? The enthusiasts' stress on subjectivity, like the late medieval view of penance and monasticism, troubles Luther because it puts the question of salvation back into the hands of a frail and doubting humanity. God, however, is merciful. He comes to us via outward means—water, bread, and wine. He pledges himself to us in these visible and tangible signs, for 'faith must have something to believe—something to which it may cling and upon which it may stand.' "[9]

Baptism is a place of refuge for the troubled and distressed soul because it encompasses the whole of the Christian's life. Already in *The Babylonian Captivity of the Church*, Luther condemns Jerome's notion of penance as "the second plank after the shipwreck of baptism as a pernicious error" (AE 36:61). This condemnation is repeated in the Large Catechism as Luther concludes that Jerome's view "takes away the value of baptism,

9 Tranvik, "Luther on Baptism," 83–84.

making of it no further use to us" (LC IV 82; K-W, p. 466). Baptism has value precisely because it embraces the entire life of the believer from font to grave and entails "daily contrition and repentance," to use the words of the Small Catechism (SC IV 12; K-W, p. 360). Luther is explicit on this point in the Large Catechism: "Thus a Christian life is nothing else than a daily baptism, begun once and continuing ever after. For we must keep at it without ceasing, always purging whatever pertains to the old Adam, so that whatever belongs to the new creature may come forth" (LC IV 65; K-W, p. 465).[10] For Luther, the medieval penitential practices are replaced by a renewed emphasis on the baptismal life as the life of repentance and faith. Confession and Absolution remain but are now envisioned in connection to Baptism and a return to the forgiveness of sins bestowed in Baptism.

10 Also note Trigg: "The circularity of the Christian life for Luther is reflected in several aspects of his theology. Conversion itself becomes, not an event, but a state to be persevered in by the Christian who must be *semper penitens.* The indivisibility of grace is another expression of the same principle; for Luther the Christian is no longer a pilgrim travelling from one degree, mode, or means of grace to another. But perhaps it is in the *simul* doctrine that the circularity of the Christian life comes to its clearest expression. A Christian never progresses beyond the need for justification because of the nature of justification itself—he remains a sinner although righteousness is imputed to him as he lives by faith. But living in faith is a continuous necessity, not a once-for-all event. Sin remains, the need for repentance and faith remains. The person who is *simul iustus et peccator,* who is living at once in two kingdoms, who is both flesh and spirit, is, in Oberman's phrase, 'man between God and the devil.' The life of faith is no complacent reflection on past victories but an armed struggle." Jonathan Trigg, *Baptism in the Theology of Martin Luther* (New York: E. J. Brill, 1994), 170.

For Further Reading and Study

Allison, C. FitzSimons. "Pastoral Care in the Light of Justification by Faith Alone." In *By Faith Alone: Essays on Justification in Honor of Gerhard O. Forde*, edited by Joseph Burgess and Marc Kolden. Grand Rapids: Eerdmans, 2004. 305–315.

Aurelius, Carl Axel. "Luther on the Psalter." *Lutheran Quarterly* (Summer 2000): 193–205.

———. "*Quo verbum dei vel cantu inter populos maneat:* The Hymns of Martin Luther." In *The Arts and Cultural Heritage of Martin Luther*, edited by Nils Holger Peterson et al. Copenhagen: University of Copenhagen, 2003. 19–34.

Arand, Charles. *That I May Be His Own: An Overview of Luther's Catechisms*. St. Louis: Concordia, 2000.

Bayer, Oswald. *Freedom in Response—Lutheran Ethics: Sources and Controversies*. Translated by Jeffrey Cayzer. Oxford: Oxford University Press, 2007.

———. *Living by Faith*. Translated by G. W. Bromiley. Grand Rapids: Eerdmans, 2003.

———. "Luther's Ethics as Pastoral Care." *Lutheran Quarterly* (Summer 1990): 125–42.

———. *Martin Luther's Theology: A Contemporary Interpretation*. Translated by Thomas Trapp. Grand Rapids: Eerdmans, 2008.

———. "God's Omnipotence." *Lutheran Quarterly* (Spring 2009): 85–102.

———. *Theology the Lutheran Way*. Translated by Jeffrey Silcock and Mark Mattes. Grand Rapids: Eerdmans, 2007.

———. "With Luther in the Present." *Lutheran Quarterly* (Spring 2007): 1–16.

Baue, Frederic W. "Luther on Preaching as Explanation and Exclamation." *Lutheran Quarterly* (Winter 1995): 405–18.

Becker, Arthur. "Luther as *Seelsorger*." In *Interpreting Luther's Legacy: Essays in Honor of Edward C. Fendt*. Edited by Fred Meuser and Stanley Schneider, 136–50. Minneapolis: Augsburg, 1969.

Bornkamm, Heinrich. *Luther in Mid-Career*. Translated by E. Theodore Bachmann. Philadelphia: Fortress Press, 1983.

Brecht, Martin. *Martin Luther: His Road to Reformation 1483–1521*. Translated by James L. Schaaf. Minneapolis: Fortress Press, 1993.

———. *Martin Luther: Shaping and Defining the Reformation*. Translated by James L. Schaaf. Minneapolis: Fortress Press, 1990.

———. *Martin Luther: The Preservation of the Church 1532–1546*. Translated by James L. Schaaf. Minneapolis: Fortress Press, 1993.

Ebeling, Gerhard. *Luthers Seelsorge: Theologie in der Vielfalt der Lebenssituationen an seinen Briefen dargestellt*. Tübigen: J. C. B. Mohr, 1997.

———. *Luther: An Introduction to His Thought*. Translated by R. A. Wilson. Philadelphia: Fortress Press, 1972.

Forde, Gerhard. "Luther's Ethics." In *A More Radical Gospel: Essays on Eschatology, Authority, Atonement, and Ecumenism*, edited by Mark C. Mattes and Steven D. Paulson, 137–58. Grand Rapids: Eerdmans, 2004.

———. *On Being a Theologian of the Cross: Reflections on Luther's Heidelberg Disputation, 1518*. Grand Rapids: Eerdmans, 1997.

———. *The Captivation of the Will: Luther vs. Erasmus on Freedom and Bondage*. Grand Rapids: Eerdmans, 2005.

———. *The Preached God: Proclamation in Word and Sacrament*. Grand Rapids: Eerdmans, 2007.

Gritsch, Eric. *The Wit of Martin Luther*. Minneapolis: Fortress Press, 2006.

Haemig, Mary Jane. "Prayer as Talking Back to God in Luther's Genesis Lectures." *Lutheran Quarterly* (Autumn 2009): 270–95.

Hagen, Kenneth. "Luther's Preaching to the Hometown Folks." In *Preaching Through the Ages: The Pieper Lectures 2003*, edited by John Maxfield, 64–87. St. Louis: Concordia Historical Institute, 2004.

Hempelmann, L. Dean. "Luther, Shepherd Under Christ." *Lutheran Theological Review* (Fall/Winter 1995): 83–93.

Hendrix, Scott. "Martin Luther's Reformation of Spirituality." *Lutheran Quarterly* (Autumn 1999): 249–70.

Heubach, Joachim. *Luthers als Seelsorge.* Erlangen: Martin-Luther-Verlag, 1991.

Hummel, Leonard. *Clothed in Nothingness: Consolation for Suffering.* Minneapolis: Fortress Press, 2003.

Ishida, Yoshiro. "Luther the Pastor." In *Piety, Politics, and Ethics: Reformation Studies in Honor of George Wolfgang Forell*, edited by Carter Lindberg, 27–37. Kirksville: The Sixteenth Century Journal Publishers, 1984.

Ivarsson, Henrik. "The Principles of Pastoral Care According to Martin Luther." *Pastoral Psychology* (February 1962): 19–25.

Iwand, Hans Joachim. *The Righteousness of Faith According to Luther.* Eugene: Wipf & Stock, 2008.

Jüngel, Eberhard. *The Freedom of a Christian: Luther's Significance for Contemporary Theology*, translated by Roy A. Harrisville. Minneapolis: Augsburg, 1988.

Keller, Rudolf. "Luther als Seelsorge." *Lutherische Kirche in der Welt.* Jahrbuch des Martin-Luther-Bundes 44 (1997), 101–18.

Kolb, Robert. *Bound Choice, Election, and Wittenberg Theological Method: From Martin Luther to the Formula of Concord.* Grand Rapids: Eerdmans, 2005.

———. *Luther and the Stories of God: Biblical Narratives as a Foundation for Christian Living.* Grand Rapids: Baker Academic Press, 2012.

———. "Luther as Seelsorge." *Concordia Journal* (January 1985): 2–9.

———. "Luther, the Master Pastor: Conrad Porta's *Pastorale Lutheri*, Handbook for Generations." *Concordia Journal* (September 1983): 179–87.

———. *Martin Luther as Prophet, Teacher, and Hero: Images of The Reformer 1520–1620.* Grand Rapids: Baker Books, 1999.

———. *Martin Luther: Confessor of the Faith.* Oxford: Oxford Press, 2009.

———, and Charles P. Arand. *The Genius of Luther's Theology: A Wittenberg Way for the Contemporary Church*. Grand Rapids: Backer Academic Press, 2008.

———. "What Benefit Does the Soul Receive from a Handful of Water? Luther's Preaching on Baptism, 1528–1539." *Concordia Journal* (October 1999): 346–63.

Krey, Philip D. W., ed. and trans. *Luther's Spirituality*. New York: Paulist Press, 2007.

Krispin, Gerald. "A Study in Luther's Pastoral Theology." *Logia* (Eastertide 2001): 13–20.

———. "The Consolation of the Resurrection in Luther." *Lutheran Theological Review* (Fall/Winter 1989–90): 37–51.

Lazareth, William. *Christians in Society: Luther, the Bible, and Social Ethics*. Minneapolis: Fortress Press, 2001.

———. *Luther on the Christian Home*. Philadelphia: Muhlenberg Press, 1960.

Leroux, Neil R. *Luther's Rhetoric: Strategies and Style from the Invocavit Sermons*. St. Louis: Concordia, 2002.

———. *Martin Luther as Comforter: Writings on Death*. Leiden: Brill, 2007.

Lose, David. "Luther and Calvin on Preaching to the Human Condition." *Lutheran Quarterly* (Autumn 1996): 281–318.

Lohse, Bernhard. *Martin Luther's Theology: Its Historical and Systematic Development*, translated by Roy A. Harrisville. Minneapolis: Fortress Press, 1999.

Mayer, Herbert T. *Pastoral Care: Its Roots and Renewal*. Atlanta: John Knox, 1979.

Meuser, Fred. *Luther the Preacher*. Minneapolis: Augsburg, 1983.

McKim, Donald, ed. *The Cambridge Companion to Martin Luther*. New York: Cambridge University Press, 2003.

McNair, Bruce G. "Luther and the Pastoral Theology of the Lord's Prayer." *Logia* (Reformation 2005): 41–46.

Mikoteit, Matthias. *Theologie und Gebet bei Luther: Untersuchungen zur Psalmenvorlesung 1532–1535*. Berlin: Walter de Gruyter, 2004.

Nebe, August. *Luther as Spiritual Advisor.* Philadelphia: Lutheran Publication Society, 1894.

Nembach, Ulrich. "*De servo arbitrio*-seelsorgerlich gelesen." In *Welthandeln Und Heilshandeln Gottes: Deus absonditus-Deus revelatus.* Veroeffentlichungen der Luther-Akademie e.V. Ratzeburg, vol. 29, edited by Joachim Heubach, 95–107. Erlangen: Martin-Luther Verlag, 1999.

Nestingen, James A. "Luther's Cultural Translation of the Catechism." *Lutheran Quarterly* (Winter 2001): 440–52.

———. "Luther on Marriage, Vocation, and the Cross." *Word & World* (Winter 2003): 31–39.

———. "The Lord's Prayer in Luther's Catechism." *Word & World* (Winter 2002): 36–48.

Ngien, Dennis. *Luther as Spiritual Advisor.* London: Paternoster, 2007.

Olmstead, Richard H. "Staking All on Faith's Object: The Art of Christian Assurance According to Martin Luther and Karl Barth." *Pro Ecclesia* (Spring 2001): 135–58.

Pahl, P. David. "A Bodily Influence in the Sacrament, in the Fathers, in Luther, in Modern Lutheranism." In *Theologia Crucis: Studies in Honour of Hermann Sasse*, edited by Henry Hamann, 61–71. Adelaide; Lutheran Publishing House, 1975.

Paulson, Steven. *Luther for Armchair Theologians.* Louisville: Westminster John Knox Press, 2004.

———. "Luther on the Hidden God." *Word & World* (Fall 1999): 363–74.

Pietsch, Stephen. "Luther Comforts a Depressed Pastor." *Lutheran Theological Journal* (December 2011): 144–55.

———. "Seelsorge: A Living Tradition in Pastoral Theology Practice." *Lutheran Theological Journal* (May 2009): 49–62.

Pless, John T. "Baptism as Consolation in Luther's Pastoral Care." *Concordia Theological Quarterly* (January 2003): 19–32.

———. *Luther on the Care for the Sick and Dying.* St. Louis: Lutheran Cancer & Hospice Society, 2007.

———. "Your Pastor Is Not Your Therapist: Private Confession—The

Ministry of Repentance and Faith." *Logia* (Eastertide 2001): 21–26.

Preus, Herman A. *A Theology to Live By: The Practical Luther for the Practicing Christian*. St. Louis: Concordia, 1977.

Reinis, Austra. *Reforming the Art of Dying: The ars moriendi in the German Reformation (1519–1528)*. Burlington, VT: Ashgate Publishing Company, 2007.

Rieth, Ricardo Willy. "Luther on Greed." *Lutheran Quarterly* (Autumn 2001): 336–51.

Rittgers, Ronald K. "Luther on Private Confession." *Lutheran Quarterly* (Autumn 2005): 312–31.

———. *The Reformation of Suffering: Pastoral Theology and Lay Piety and Late Medieval and Early Modern Germany*. Oxford: Oxford University Press, 2012.

———. *The Reformation of the Keys: Confession, Conscience, and Authority in Sixteenth-Century Germany*. Cambridge: Harvard University Press, 2004.

Russell, W. R. "Luther, Prayer, and the Reformation." *Word & World* (Winter 2002): 49–54.

———. *Luther's Theological Testament: The Schmalkald Articles*. Minneapolis: Fortress Press, 1995.

———. "Prayer: The Practical Focus of Luther's Theology." In *Let Christ Be Christ*, edited by Daniel Harmelink, 293–98. Huntington Beach, CA: Tentatio Press, 1999.

Sauter, Gerhard. "Luther on the Resurrection." *Lutheran Quarterly* (Summer 2001): 195–216.

Schild, Maurice. "Luther as Comforter." In *Perspectives on Martin Luther*, edited by Mark Worthing, 9–20. Adelaide: Luther Seminary, 1996.

———. "Praying the Catechism and Defrocking the Devil—Aspects of Luther's Spirituality." *Lutheran Theological Journal* (August 1976): 48–56.

Schumacher, William W. *Who Do I Say That You Are? Anthropology and the Theology of Theosis in the Finnish School of Tuomo Mannermaa*. Eugene, Oregon: Wipf & Stock, 2010.

Siggins, Ian K. *Martin Luther's Doctrine of Christ.* New Haven: Yale University Press, 1970.

Slenczka, Reinhard. "Luther's Care of Souls for Our Time." *Concordia Theological Quarterly* (January 2003): 33–63.

———. *Ziel und Ende: Einweisung in die christliche Endzeiterwartung: Der Herr ist Nahe.* Neuendettelsau: Freimund-Verlag, 2008.

Smith, Ralph E. *Luther, Ministry, and Ordination in the Early Reformation Church.* New York: Peter Lang, 1996.

Spinks, Bryan. "Luther's Timely Theology of Unilateral Baptism." *Lutheran Quarterly* (Spring 1995): 23–46.

Steiger, Johann Anselm. "The *communio idiomatum* as the Axle and Motor of Luther's Theology." *Lutheran Quarterly* (Summer 2000): 125–58.

Strohl, Jane E. "Luther and the Word of Consolation." *Lutheran Theological Seminary Bulletin* (Winter 1987): 23–34.

———. "Luther's 'Fourteen Consolations'." *Lutheran Quarterly* (Summer 1989): 169–82.

Tappert, Theodore, ed. *Luther's Letters of Spiritual Counsel.* Philadelphia: Westminster Press, 1955.

Tinder, Galen. "Luther's Theology of Christian Suffering." *Dialog* (Spring 1986): 108–13.

Torvend, Samuel. *Luther and the Hungry Poor: Gathered Fragments.* Minneapolis: Fortress Press, 2008.

Tranvik, Mark. "Luther on Baptism." *Lutheran Quarterly* (Spring 1999): 75–90.

Trigg, Jonathan. *Baptism in the Theology of Martin Luther.* New York: E. J. Brill, 1994.

Vatja, Vilmos. *Luther on Worship*, translated by U. Leopold. Philadelphia: Muhlenberg Press, 1958.

Wengert, Timothy J., ed. *Harvesting Martin Luther's Reflections on Theology, Ethics, and the Church.* Grand Rapids: Eerdmans, 2004.

———. *Martin Luther's Catechisms: Forming the Faith.* Minneapolis: Fortress Press, 2009.

———. "Peace, Peace . . . Cross, Cross: Reflections on How Martin Luther Relates the Theology of the Cross to Suffering." *Theology Today* (July 2002): 190–205.

———. *The Pastoral Luther: Essays on Martin Luther's Practical Theology.* Grand Rapids: Eerdmans, 2009.

Wicks, Jared, S. J. "Applied Theology at the Deathbed: Luther and the Late-Medieval Tradition of the *Ars moriendi.*" *Gregorianum* (number 2 1998), 345–68.

Wilson, H. S. "Luther on Preaching as God Speaking." *Lutheran Quarterly* (Spring 2005): 63–76.

———. *The Speaking God: Luther's Theology of Preaching.* Madras: United Evangelical Lutheran Churches in India, 1982.

Wingren, Gustaf. *Luther on Vocation*, translated by C. Rasmussen. Philadelphia: Muhlenberg Press, 1957.

Wright, William J. *Martin Luther's Understanding of God's Two Kingdoms: A Response to the Challenge of Skepticism.* Grand Rapids: Baker Academic, 2009.